Old Stories
for a
New Time

JAMES LIMBURG

John Knox Press
ATLANTA

Library of Congress Cataloging in Publication Data
Limburg, James, 1935-
   Old stories for a new time.

   Includes bibliographical references.
   1. Story-telling in Christian education. 2. Bible.
O.T.–Homiletical use. 3. Story-telling (Christian theology) I. Title.
BV1534.3.L55 1983   207   82-49019
ISBN 0-8042-0148-X

John Knox Press
Atlanta, Georgia 30365

To my mother
who read us stories
And my father
who still tells them

PREFACE

The setting was the basement of a white frame church, located on the prairies of southwestern Minnesota. I had been teaching a series of classes on the Old Testament. Our topic for the evening was the story of Jonah.

"Now if we rightly understand this story," I asked the group, "who is Jonah?"

"Israel," someone suggested, and we spoke of ancient Israel and its reluctance to take up the challenge to become a light to the nations. "The church," suggested another, and we talked about evangelism and the missionary task of the people of God.

Then, when the discussion seemed to have come to an end, an older farmer who had been present at all our sessions but who had not yet said a word, spoke: "I think," he said, "that Jonah is me." He explained why, and others added their own comments. Then we all knew that the old story had spoken to our new time.

Since that evening, I have listened to the story of Jonah, as well as to others of the stories discussed in these pages, in a variety of settings. These have included college and seminary classrooms, church basements, sanctuaries, and educational units, camps, retreat centers, convents, even the assembly room of a city police station, where two dozen patrolmen were furthering their education through an extension course. In each of these settings I have seen the same thing happen: the impact of the story moves from "they" (Israel) to "us" (the church) and then to "me." Time and again I have come away from such settings astonished at the power with which these old stories are charged, and at the way in which that power leaps across the gap from then to now.

It is my hope that this book will be useful in contexts as varied as those in which the material took shape. I have intended it to be used wherever people are interested in listening to the stories which the Old Testament tells. It must be read, of course, alongside the Bible. I suggest that because of its clarity and freshness, the *Good News Bible (Today's English Version*, GNB) be used. Whenever possible, the biblical texts should be read aloud.

I should like to acknowledge three debts. The first is to the Jewish writer and storyteller, Elie Wiesel. A comment which he added to an old Hasidic tale sparked the idea for a college seminar on stories: "God made man because he loves stories" (see chapter 1). When I have taught these stories in classes with academic requirements, we have always read two of Wiesel's books: *Night*, which tells of his experiences as a boy in the concentration camps, and *Souls on Fire*, a collection of Hasidic stories. I know of no writer who can retell old stories for a new time as effectively as does Elie Wiesel.

The second debt is to Claus Westermann, for many years Professor of Old Testament at Heidelberg University in Germany. His expositions of Old Testament narratives, particularly those in Genesis, are masterfully done. He, too, always enables the old story to address a new time. His books, *What Does the Old Testament Say About God?* and *Elements of Old Testament Theology* indicate how the story theme can unify the variety of materials which the Bible contains (see chapter 1).

Then I must thank those who have listened to these stories with me over the past decade or so: students in classes at Augustana College in Sioux Falls and at Luther Northwestern Seminary in St. Paul; pastors at conferences and in continuing education courses; participants in Sunday morning adult education classes; people of the church, from nuns to policemen, in a whole variety of situations. Their interest and insights have provided the context and the commentary which have helped me to hear what these stories have to say.

I want to acknowledge with gratitude the encouragement of Richard A. Ray at the beginning of this project and the careful and thoughtful editing of Joan Crawford at its conclusion.

Finally, some lines from a storyteller when he had completed his task:

> So I too will here end my story.
> If it is well told and to the point,
>   that is what I myself desired;
> if it is poorly done and mediocre,
>   that was the best I could do.
>
> 2 Maccabees 15:37-38

James Limburg
Luther Northwestern Theological Seminary

CONTENTS

CHAPTER 1

A Time for Stories

Ours is a time ready for stories.

In the opening chapter of his best-selling book, *On Being a Christian,* Hans Küng makes the following observation:

> In the midst of the Vietnam war, Erich Segal's *Love Story* was the first token of a reaction. . . . Instead of protests and peace marches we now have the idylls of private happiness. Even in the most modern literature the old preferences are again evident: for narrative, biography and autobiography, for stories generally.[1]

The book by Segal appeared in 1970. Wearied by the struggles with civil rights at home, worn out by the perplexities of a war abroad, the American people were ready for an uncomplicated tale about romance on a college campus. Soon *Love Story* captured the imagination of lovers everywhere. It was made into a movie. People listened to the title song on radios and stereo phonographs and whistled it as they worked. That book, suggests Küng, signaled the beginning of a shift in literary taste. A tired and torn world was ready for "narrative, biography and autobiography, for stories generally."

A Time for Stories

In 1976, Alex Haley published *Roots*. In it he told of his search for his own ancestry and how he thus discovered something about his own identity. The book became a bestseller and was made into a television series. A whole nation became caught up in the story of one man's search for his roots. This man's story inspired others to investigate their own family histories. The Bicentennial celebration in the United States in 1976, which recalled the story of the nation, gave further impetus to the quest for "roots." More and more Americans have been making trips back to the "old country" to walk on the land and meet the people who live in the places from which their ancestors came. In this relatively young nation, the first generations had wanted to forget the old ways and quickly embraced the new American language and culture. But nowadays, especially since the Bicentennial, we see a revival of ethnic names, food, and festivals, celebrating the Polish or German, Irish or Dutch, Norwegian or Swedish roots of communities across the United States. One wise college teacher whom I know begins his course in the history of western civilization by having his students investigate their own family histories. They learn something of their own stories before getting into the story of the civilization of which they are a part. Every person asks at some point, "Who am I?" One way of finding an answer to this question is by discovering the story of which I am a part. The "roots" phenomenon, given a label by Haley and given encouragement by the Bicentennial celebration, is an indication that ours is a time ready to discover stories.

On Sunday, July 2, 1978, the United Press International carried the following report:

> Here is the year's most surprising theatrical success story: Alec McCowen is reciting St. Mark's Gospel. That's all. McCowen strolls out to an almost bare stage in casual clothes, speaks a quiet introduction and for two hours delivers from memory the entire King James Version of the Gospel according to Mark.[2]

Time magazine reported on McCowen's success under the heading, "Telling Triumph":

> The operative word for McCowen is tell. He tells Mark's story, he does not intone it. He clears away the ponderousness and singsong preachiness of centuries of Bible reading to rediscover the urgent, living voice of a man who is recounting nearly contemporary events, many of them derived from eyewitness accounts.[3]

One actor, alone on the stage, packed theaters in England and in the United States. He retold a story, which had been written down almost two thousand years earlier. The crowds came to hear him and/or to hear the story which he told. The McCowen-Mark phenomenon would suggest that ours is a time ready to hear stories.

The most discussed television program in the United States in 1980 was undoubtedly the Friday evening serial, "Dallas." Millions watched each week, following the fortunes (and misfortunes) of the Ewing family of Texas. When the main character, J.R. Ewing, was wounded by a bullet in the springtime, the question, "Who shot J.R.?" was discussed over coffee cups and in internationally circulated news magazines throughout the summer. What sort of program is "Dallas" and why has it evoked so much interest? A biblical scholar trained in form-criticism would label it a "family story," complete with patriarch and matriarch, children and granchildren. Like the stories in Genesis 12–50, the most important events in "Dallas" are those which take place within the family. Young people fall in love and marry, babies are born, old people reminisce about times past. There is also rivalry between brothers, jealousy among wives, rebellion against parents. Why has this program been so popular? It is a family story, with the problems and possibilities of family life exaggerated. Since we all live in families, we can perhaps see something of ourselves (or at least, something of other members of the tribe!) in the characters of "Dallas." The "Dallas" phenomenon suggests that ours is a time ready to hear family stories.

We could cite further examples in support of the assertion that ours is a time ready for stories. The academy-award winning motion pictures for 1979 and 1980 did not deal with global or cosmic issues but were family stories: *Kramer vs. Kramer,* which focused on divorce and the relationships between parents and a child, and *Ordinary People,* which told the story of how a family dealt with an accidental drowning. The 1981 winner, *Chariots of Fire,* was an old fashioned success story, telling about the struggles of two individuals as they prepared to compete in the 1924 Olympics. On the radio, the old dramas may be heard once again; one can purchase cassette recordings of old radio shows from the 40s or borrow them at the public library. People are interested in hearing these stories once again. In the home, a teenager is found escaping from the sounds of rock groups like "Kiss" or "Rush" because of discovering the Narnia stories of C.S. Lewis. A pastor who has been living in Germany tells of the impact of the story form; while his congregation had been very much aware of the events of the Nazi era, it was the story of one family as told in the television film, *Holocaust,* which precipitated the most intense discussion of those years.

Finally, the "American Scene" entry in *Time* magazine for August 3, 1981, reports on storytelling at the Opera House in Rockport, Maine, and includes the following comment:

> It would be too much of a storyteller's exaggeration to suggest that in the middle of an electronic giant's blink—presto!—the art of the storyteller is about to recapture the castle. But certainly more things are happening on the stage of the Rockport Opera House, and elsewhere, than the programmers of the age of television ever dreamed of. This year of the First Annual North Atlantic Festival is also the year of the First Storytelling Festival in New York City, the Second Annual Storytelling Festival in St. Louis and the Third Annual New Mexico Storytelling Festival in Albuquerque. Something called the National Association for the Preservation and Perpetuation of Storytelling in Jonesboro, Tenn., numbers over 800 members. Storytelling has become a respectable course in the college curriculum, without its old academic euphemism, the "Oral Literary Tradition."[4]

But such is enough. Signals from a variety of sources suggest that Professor Küng is right. The "old preferences . . . for narrative, biography and autobiography, for stories generally" are again evident. Ours is a time ready for stories.

The Old Testament Tells a Story

Claus Westermann's book, *Elements of Old Testament Theology,* offers a synthesis of a lifetime of study of the Old Testament. In the opening chapter, Westermann discusses the problem of the organization of a theology of the Old Testament. He writes:

> If we wish to describe what the Old Testament as a whole says about God, we must start by looking at the way the Old Testament presents itself, something everyone can recognize: "The Old Testament tells a story" (G. von Rad).[5]

A few pages later he continues:

> The theology of the Old Testament thus remains determined in every aspect by the outline of a story entrusted to us which includes the occurrence of God speaking and the response of those who experience these events.[6]

If "story" is central to the Old Testament, what sort of story does the Old Testament tell?

We can start with one of its central texts. In chapter 26 of Deuteronomy, we find some instructions, telling how a farmer in Israel was to go about worshiping the Lord. He was to fill a basket with the firstfruits of the harvest and then take it to the place of worship. As he gave the basket to the priest in charge, he would confess his faith. That confession took the form of telling the story of what God had done for him and for his people. Note that this story starts by telling about "they," then shifts to "us" (that farmer had never been in Egypt, but he so identifies with the story that it becomes his own) and, finally, "I," as he links his own life to the story of what God had done for his ancestors:

> "My ancestor was a wandering Aramean, who took his family to Egypt to live. They were few in number when they went there, but they became a large and powerful nation. The Egyptians treated us harshly and forced us to work as slaves. Then we cried out to the LORD, the God of our ancestors. He heard us and saw our suffering, hardship, and misery. By his great power and strength he rescued us from Egypt. He worked miracles and wonders, and caused terrifying things to happen. He brought us here and gave us this rich and fertile land. So now I bring to the LORD the first part of the harvest that he has given me." (Deut. 26:5–10, GNB)

When this farmer spoke about God, he told a story. He recalled how God had delivered the Israelites from Egypt, and then acknowledged that God had continued to bless him, by giving him a good life in a rich and fertile land.

That farmer's creed started with Jacob, the "wandering Aramean," and continued through the experience in Egypt, the wandering in the wilderness, and the entry into the promised land. The biblical books of Genesis through Joshua then expand upon that story, but what of the books that follow after Joshua?

At this point, it is necessary to say something about how contemporary biblical scholarship views the makeup of the Old Testament.

Most often, the first five books of the Bible are considered together. In the Hebrew Bible, for example, these books make up the first division, called the "Torah" (a word usually translated as "law," but better understood as "instruction"). We can also take as the first section in the Old Testament the first four books, Genesis through Numbers. Here we have an account of the story of God's people beginning with the origin of all things and continuing through the wilderness wanderings. Since it was most likely put into its final form by priests living with their people in exile in Babylon (587–539 B.C.), it may be called the "Priestly History." This "Priestly History" made use of very old materials (which scholars label "J," for Jahwe or Yahweh, and "E," for Elohim), supplementing and editing them to present this account of what happened between God and God's people.

The next books in the Bible—Deuteronomy, Joshua, Judges, 1 and 2 Samuel, 1 and 2 Kings—tell the story of God's people from the time just before the settling of the land in about 1240 B.C. to the time when the citizens of Judah are in exile in Babylon. We have skipped the book of Ruth in this listing because in the Hebrew Bible that book is found in the last division of the Bible. This section, from Deuteronomy through 2 Kings, continues the story of God and people. It also appears to have been put in its final form (again making use of older materials) during the time of the exile and is called the "Deuteronomistic History."

There is yet a third unified historical work in the Old Testament. If you look at the beginning of 1 Chronicles, you see that the first word is "Adam." Here begins the "Chronicler's History," a telling of the story which starts at the very beginning, with Adam, and continues into the time of Ezra and Nehemiah, in the 400s B.C. It includes the books of 1 and 2 Chronicles, Ezra, and Nehemiah.

The Old Testament tells a story. There are, in fact, three major historical works which tell the story of God and God's people. Like the Gospels at the beginning of the New Testament, each of these tellings has its own particular characteristics, its own point (and points) to make. Each has its own way of speaking about God. But all three speak about God by telling the story of God and God's relationship to the people.

The Old Testament tells a story. This helps us to tie together the books from Genesis through Nehemiah. But what of the rest? The other parts of the Old Testament can be related to the story, too. We have noted Westermann's statement:

> The theology of the Old Testament thus remains determined in every aspect by the outline of a story entrusted to us which includes the occurrence of God speaking and the response of those who experience these events.[7]

The prophetic books present us with the "occurrence of God speaking." Here we have collections of words from God to people, delivered by God's messengers, in this way inserted into the story. Since the story is always about God and people, and never just about God alone, the Bible also presents us with something of "the response of those who experience these events." That response is found in the book of Psalms where we hear the voices of God's people giving praise for what God has done and for what God is, but also bringing their troubles and complaints to God. Other books, such as Proverbs, Job, and Ecclesiastes, may also be seen as part of that response. When we look at the biblical materials in this way, we can see how "story" integrates the variety of material which makes up the Old Testament.

The story does not end with the last book of the Old Testament, however. For the Christian, it continues in those writings which make up the New Testament. We discover, in fact, that at the core of the Christian faith is a story, told in four different versions in the Gospels.

The centrality of "story" for the Christian faith has been eloquently expressed in a recent Presbyterian statement of faith:

> JESUS CHRIST STANDS AT THE CENTER OF A STORY.
> In the biblical story God moves with Israel and the church
> as Father, Son, and Holy Spirit,
> to establish his just and loving rule in the world.
> That story is still unfolding
> and in faith we make it our own.
> It forms our memory and our hope.
> It tells us who we are and what we are to do.
> To retell it is to declare what we believe.
>
> GOD IS AT WORK BEYOND OUR STORY.
> We are confident God is not confined to the story we can tell.
> From the story we know God is active among all peoples.
> We believe God works beyond our imagining
> throughout the universe.[8]

We conclude this section with a quotation from theologian Joseph Sittler. In an interview he describes the role of the minister or priest as the "storyteller of the great tradition." After giving a summary of "the story," which begins with the Old Testament and continues through the New Testament, he says the following:

> I believe the Christian faith because I know of no other story which, in its tragedy and pathos, its joy and its delight—no other story which has expressed life both in its disorganized and in its organized activity with anything like the very veracity, the vivacity, the actuality and the ductility to all human life that characterizes this story.[9]

Central to the Old and New Testaments is a story. As these two quotations indicate, the Christian faith itself can be described in terms of a story, too.

The Old Testament Tells Stories

The Old Testament tells a story. It is also true, of course, that the Old Testament tells stories. Now let us turn from an examination of the biblical material to some reflection on your own experience.

How did you first learn anything about the Christian faith?

If you grew up in a Christian home, chances are that your earliest understanding of what it meant to be a Christian came through stories. Perhaps your mother or father read "Bible stories" to you out of a book which had colored pictures of David standing over Goliath, Daniel in the lion's den, Jesus the Good Shepherd. Maybe you can still recall sitting in a Sunday school class where the teacher told those stories in a way which made them interesting, even exciting. Perhaps that whole world, populated by heroes such as Gideon and Samson, David and Daniel, Jesus and Paul, was very real to you. It could be that you sang, "I love to tell the story" as a child in a small church somewhere, and you sang it with honesty and gusto.

What happens to your encounter with those stories, as you grow up? The stories are still being told by parents in homes and by heroic Sunday school teachers who try to compete with the colored cartoons offered on television the morning before. Often the encounter with those stories stops when the student finishes the elementary grades and moves into junior high school. There the curriculum concerns itself with courses in basic Christian doctrines, teachings of other denominations, and the like.

What would happen if you returned to some of these old stories now, as an adult? What might you discover, if you gave them a fresh hearing? What could take place if you gave these old stories as much attention as you give to an academy-award winning movie, or to a one-hour drama on television, or to the latest issue of *Newsweek* or *Time*? What would you find, if you listened to these old stories, related them to the one great story which the whole Bible tells and to your own story as well?

I suggest that you would find these stories interesting, perhaps even exciting. It is possible that through these ancient words you might detect a directing word. It could be that you would discover for yourself why these stories

are in a collection of writings which God's people have always valued so great-
ly that they have called the collection Holy Scripture.

A Conclusion and A Story

To this point we have argued, first of all, that the "story" form is enjoying
a new popularity in our time. One could say that stories have always been a
favorite form of both oral and written discourse. But the evidence gathered in
the first part of this chapter suggests that there is a new readiness for stories in
our own time.

Secondly, we have noted that "story" is central to the Old Testament. To
be sure, that collection of writings contains a great variety of genres: laws,
proverbs, prophetic sayings, songs, and many more. However, that which integrates the whole is a continuous narrative, a story. We have also reflected
briefly on the important role that stories from both Testaments have played in
the transmission of the faith from generation to generation.

Now to draw a conclusion: if it is true that ours is a time ready for stories,
and if it is also true that the Old Testament tells a story and tells stories, then
it follows that ours ought to be a time ready to give a new hearing to what the
Old Testament has to say. The chapters which follow will attempt to facilitate
that hearing, allowing these old stories to address a new time.

At the beginning of one of his books, Elie Wiesel retells an old Hasidic
story and then adds a comment of his own:

> When the great Rabbi Israel Baal Shem-Tov saw misfortune threatening the
> Jews it was his custom to go into a certain part of the forest to meditate. There
> he would light a fire, say a special prayer, and the miracle would be accom-
> plished and the misfortune averted.
>
> Later, when his disciple, the celebrated Magid of Mezritch, had occasion, for the
> same reason, to intercede with heaven, he would go to the same place in the
> forest and say: "Master of the Universe, listen! I do not know how to light the
> fire, but I am still able to say the prayer." and again the miracle would be
> accomplished.
>
> Still later, Rabbi Moshe-Leib of Sasov, in order to save his people once more,
> would go into the forest and say: "I do not know how to light the fire, I do not
> know the prayer, but I know the place and this must be sufficient." It was
> sufficient and the miracle was accomplished.
>
> Then it fell to Rabbi Israel of Rizhyn to overcome misfortune. Sitting in his
> armchair, his head in his hands, he spoke to God: "I am unable to light the fire

and I do not know the prayer; I cannot even find the place in the forest. All I can do is to tell the story, and this must be sufficient." And it was sufficient.

God made man because he loves stories.[10]

It should not be surprising that we human beings like stories. After all, we have been created in the image of God and, according to this tale, God likes stories, too!

CHAPTER 2

Listening to the Stories

We begin this chapter with a question: which gets you more involved, watching a story on television or listening to one on the radio?

Before answering the question think back for a moment to the pre-television era. These were the days of the radio mystery programs. In the evening families would sit around the Philco floor-model radio and listen to them. There were programs with names like "Inner Sanctum," or "I Love a Mystery," or "Lights Out," or "Suspense." One of them opened with the sound of a door squeaking and then an eerie voice announcing, "This is your host, Raymond. . . ." Another suggested that the appropriate setting for listening was with all lights turned out. Yet another introduced each new story with the words, "Listen to a tale well-calculated to keep you in [sound of a gong] SUSPENSE."

Imagine yourself alone, at night, with only the green-yellow light of the radio dial illuminating the room. The story begins:

How did it happen? You rub your eyes and wake up to find yourself in what appears to be the basement of a huge old house. The walls are damp, and the only light comes from a single bulb, hanging by a cord from the ceiling. Suddenly the hum of the electric appliances stops and the light goes out. The house is strangely silent and the darkness is total. You hear a doorknob click. A door opens. You feel a cold draft on the back of your neck. Then you hear the sound of footsteps, uneven, slow, and along with those footsteps an odd tapping noise, like that of a cane or walking stick. The steps are coming closer, closer . . .

If you are old enough to remember such programs, you know that hearing a story on the radio could get you more terrified, more involved, than watching a mystery on television. Why? Because in the case of the radio drama, the video component is not limited to a nineteen or twenty-one inch screen. The video is furnished by your own imagination. You visualize that old basement, you feel the dampness, and you can imagine what sort of creature is responsible for the tapping and the uneven footsteps.

Someone has called television a "cool" medium. As you sit before the set, all is laid out before you: the sights, the sounds. But radio is a "hot" medium. As you listen to a tale well told, your imagination goes into action, furnishing the video component as the action develops.

Telling Stories

Storytelling is also a "hot" medium, in that the imagination of the hearer is fully engaged. In the case of a live storyteller, the engagement is even more complete, because the storyteller can watch the audience, vary techniques when the interest lags, stretch out a point of suspense to the very last moment.

One of the best storytellers I have heard was a salesman for a magazine publishing company. I was teaching in a small midwestern high school at the time and one of my colleagues said, "Don't miss today's assembly program. You'll hear a master storyteller."

The purpose of that program was to motivate three or four hundred students, from grades seven through twelve, to sell magazines. Some of the profits were to be used to buy new playground equipment for the school.

The setting for the speech that afternoon was an impossible one. It was springtime, and the weather was unseasonably warm. The students were crammed into an old-fashioned study hall, two in a desk, some standing along the walls, some sitting on the window ledges, some on the floor. Who could hold the attention of such a mob? Who would dare enter such an arena? The image called to mind was that of Daniel about to enter the lions' den.

Then he walked in. The storyteller. He was built for addressing large groups, with a huge chest and a deep, Orson Welles kind of voice. He began with a story, "Let me tell you about the stubbornest mule in Missouri, and the greatest mule-trainer in the world. ..." He followed with an-other, then another. He had his audience laughing, and at the end of each story, it was perfectly quiet. They were with him, eager for his next words. Then he would make his pitch, "Sell those magazines, and you'll have some new playground equipment out on that schoolyard!" He would continue with information about how to go about the task, but then, as soon as he sensed a bit of fidgeting in the audience, it was back to the stories. He would get a laugh, then another, and another. Then more instruction, and back to a story or two. He played his audience like a master bass fisherman with a prize catch on the end of the line, increasing the tension, relaxing it, pausing, and then reeling in.

Good storytellers may be found in all sorts of places. I recall listening to stories on Saturday nights, in a small country store. The men would sit on benches which were near the heat register in the floor in the middle of the store. Most of them were farmers, wearing bib overalls and a wide variety of caps and hats. A few of us young boys would sit around the outside of the circle and listen. In the group of a dozen or so, two or three were good story-tellers. The tales had to do with events which took place in the past week or weeks. Each one would call to mind another. They would focus on people that everyone knew: the town banker who was a miser, the slow-witted section foreman on the railroad who was the butt of a hundred pranks, the preacher, the traveling salesman. The good storytellers recalled mostly ordinary events, shaping them into a form which held the interest of the hearers, and which usually resulted in causing laughter. The novelist Frederick Manfred once gave some advice to a group of aspiring writers: "If you want to learn how to use words," he said, "listen to smart farmers talk. They know how to tell stories. Their language is the best." He meant, I think, that the language used in such settings as the country store on Saturday night was close to the earth, concrete, pictorial.

How should a story be told? Martin Buber tells an old Hasidic story—about how to tell a story:

> A rabbi, whose grandfather had been a disciple of the Baal Shem, was asked to tell a story. "A story," he said, "must be told in such a way that it constitutes help in itself." And he told: "My grandfather was lame. Once they asked him to tell a story about his teacher. And he related how the holy Baal Shem used to hop and dance while he prayed. My grandfather rose as he spoke, and he was so swept away by his story that he himself began to hop and dance to show how

the master had done. From that hour on he was cured of his lameness. That's the way to tell a story!"[1]

Where are the storytellers today? They are still around and about, although our modern style of life with entertainment brought into each home is conspiring against them. In our time, they are perhaps most often to be found during coffee breaks at work. The time is short, and therefore the stories must be short. Most will take the form of the short humorous anecdote. In a group of a half dozen or so, there will usually be one who is an especially good storyteller. Listen to that person. Watch for the sense of timing, the building of tension, and the release of it. Listen for the historic present when past events are being narrated, "I'm sitting in the boat and I hear this strange noise. . . ." Listen for direct discourse: "And so Ole says, 'Now Lena, you never told me that before!' " Notice that the language will be vivid, concrete, specific.

The title of this chapter is "*listening* to the stories." It could have been "*interpreting* the stories," but the word "listening" was chosen intentionally for our approach to the stories in the Bible. These stories were designed to be heard. They were told orally for years, sometimes for centuries. Then they were written down. They were heard, not read, for hundreds of years; printed Bibles were not available. Thus when we approach these stories we shall want to listen for the devices of a storyteller, rather than watch for the techniques of the writer.

What Is a Story?

Before proceeding to listen to a story from the Bible, we should be clear on a matter of definition. What is a story?

First of all, it is helpful to distinguish between a story and a report. A report, as we are using the term here, is the relating of a series of events, without attention to form. Think, for example, of a child who goes with her third-grade class to the zoo. She comes home, bursts in the door, finds her mother in the kitchen, and begins to tell about her experiences:

> We got on the bus, and then we got our tickets, and then we got to the zoo. We saw the monkeys and then the giraffes and then the elephants. Then the train came off the track and tipped over. Then we saw the birds and the snakes . . .

A report is simply a linking together of a series of events which have happened. The characteristic linking device is "and then." A report presupposes a close relationship between the one making the report and the one listening to it. A mother will be interested in hearing her daughter tell about the zoo. Two lovers who have been separated will be interested in hearing everything that happened while they were apart. However, if a husband, who has just made a business trip to Chicago, begins to tell about that trip during the coffee break at work in the same way in which he has reported all to his loving wife, his colleagues will soon become bored and find an excuse to get back to their jobs.

What, then is the difference between a report and a story? Consider this account of the trip to the zoo:

> The most terrible thing happened at the zoo today! We got our tickets, got on the bus, and started out by going to see the monkeys. We walked past the cages where the monkeys are, and were looking at the giraffe. Suddenly we heard a tremendous crash. We looked, and the train which runs through the zoo had derailed. One of the cars tipped over right in front of us!

The difference between the two accounts is that first sentence, which introduces a certain suspense or tension into the story. The listener wonders, "What was the terrible thing that happened at the zoo?" The tension is increased with the sentence, "We heard a tremendous crash," and so the interest is sustained, until the tension is resolved when the teller gives an account of the derailed train and all that happened in connection with the accident.

A good storyteller knows how to introduce tension, build it up, and then release it, at just the right moment. Our businessman back from Chicago might sustain the interest of his colleagues if he begins, "A funny thing happened to me on the way to Chicago. . . ." Since most storytelling that we hear today is in the form of a short humorous anecdote or joke, consider this example:

A pastor was conducting a children's sermon and asked all the children to come forward and sit at the front of the church. When they were all settled down, he began, "All right now, boys and girls, tell me. What is it that has four legs, a bushy tail, and runs up and down trees?" (Here the tension is introduced. We can imagine the situation, and know that it is a potentially embarrassing one. Children are unpredictable. How will the question be answered?)

There is silence. No one answers. (The tension is increased. What will the answer be?)

The pastor tries again, "Think hard now, boys and girls. What is it that has four legs, a bushy tail, puts nuts in its cheeks, and runs up and down trees?"

Again there is silence. The pastor is getting nervous. His collar feels too tight. He decides to give it one more try. (More increase of tension. . . .)

"Come now. Four legs. A bushy tail. Runs up and down trees." (Now the tension has been stretched to the maximum. The listeners are attentive, waiting for the resolution in the form of the "punch line.")

Finally one small boy puts up his hand and volunteers, "I really think it is a squirrel, but I suppose the answer is Jesus." With this the tension is released, the answer evokes laughter, and the story is at an end.

What does this have to do with stories in the Bible?

Professor Westermann has provided this definition of a story:

> What is a story? A story tells of something which has happened, beginning with a point of tension and finally leading to a resolution of that tension.[2]

As we listen to stories from the Bible, we shall try to identify the point of tension, and then look for the resolution of that tension. For an example, note the following from the first chapter of 1 Samuel:

> There was a man named Elkanah, from the tribe of Ephraim, who lived in the town of Ramah in the hill country of Ephraim. . . . Elkanah had two wives, Hannah and Peninnah. Peninnah had children, but Hannah did not. (vss.1–2, GNB)

There, with the last phrase, the tension is introduced. The question is raised: will Hannah ever have a child? How will she get along? During the course of the story the tension is intensified, telling how Elkanah favored Peninnah, when meat was divided up:

> And even though he loved Hannah very much he would give her only one share, because the LORD had kept her from having children. Peninnah, her rival, would torment and humiliate her. (vss. 5–6, GNB)

The story continues with Hannah's visit to the temple and her prayer for a child. Then the tension is resolved when the story says,

> So it was that she became pregnant and gave birth to a son. (vs. 20)

So the biblical stories are shaped, moving from tension to resolution of tension, to introduction of new tension.

A Story About a Father and His Son

To provide an example of how we go about listening to a story from the Bible, we shall turn to the story of Abraham and Isaac in Genesis 22:

[1]After these things God tested Abraham, and said to him, "Abraham!" And he said, "Here am I." [2]He said, "Take your son, your only son Isaac, whom you love, and go to the land of Moriah, and offer him there as a burnt offering upon one of the mountains of which I shall tell you." [3]So Abraham rose early in the morning, saddled his ass, and took two of his young men with him, and his son Isaac; and he cut the wood for the burnt offering, and arose and went to the place of which God had told him. [4]On the third day Abraham lifted up his eyes and saw the place afar off. [5]Then Abraham said to his young men, "Stay here with the ass; I and the lad will go yonder and worship, and come again to you." [6]And Abraham took the wood of the burnt offering, and laid it on Isaac his son; and he took in his hand the fire and the knife. So they went both of them together. [7]And Isaac said to his father Abraham, "My father!" And he said, "Here am I, my son." He said, "Behold, the fire and the wood; but where is the lamb for a burnt offering?" [8]Abraham said, "God will provide himself the lamb for a burnt offering, my son." So they went both of them together.

[9]When they came to the place of which God had told him, Abraham built an altar there, and laid the wood in order, and bound Isaac his son, and laid him on the altar, upon the wood. [10]Then Abraham put forth his hand, and took the knife to slay his son. [11]But the angel of the LORD called to him from heaven, and said, "Abraham, Abraham!" And he said, "Here am I." [12]He said, "Do not lay your hand on the lad or do anything to him; for now I know that you fear God, seeing you have not withheld your son, your only son, from me." [13]And Abraham lifted up his eyes and looked, and behold, behind him was a ram, caught in a thicket by his horns; and Abraham went and took the ram, and offered it up as a burnt offering instead of his son. [14]So Abraham called the name of that place The LORD will provide; as it is said to this day, "On the mount of the LORD it shall be provided."

[15]And the angel of the LORD called to Abraham a second time from heaven, [16]and said, "By myself I have sworn, says the LORD, because you have done this, and have not withheld your son, your only son, [17]I will indeed bless you, and I will multiply your descendants as the stars of heaven and as the sand which is on the seashore. And your descendants shall possess the gate of their enemies, [18]and by your descendants shall all the nations of the earth bless themselves, because you have obeyed my voice." [19]So Abraham returned to his young men, and they arose and went together to Beer-sheba; and Abraham dwelt at Beer-sheba. (Gen. 22:1-19)

While there is no rigid method which can be applied to every text, we can approach the story as follows:

1. The first question to be asked in approaching any text from the Bible is: *what is the unit?* That is, where does the text begin, and where does it end?

For some stories this is easy. The stories of Ruth, Esther, and Jonah, for example, are set apart in the Bible as books which bear those names.

For others, the task is not so simple. The account given in Genesis 22 is part of a larger collection of stories which involve Abraham (Gen. 12–25) and Isaac (Gen. 21–35). We could deal with all of that material, but it is also possible to focus on one incident from those chapters, such as that related in Genesis 22.

The beginning of this story is clearly indicated, with the expression "After these things . . ." indicating that something new is starting. But where does the unit end? As we read through the story, verse 14 seems like a possible ending. It could be that the story once ended there, and when it was incorporated into the whole of the biblical material about Abraham, verses 15–19 were added as an explanatory comment, tying the story in with the promise to Abraham given in chapter 12. Verse 20 provides us with a clue: there we find the same expression, "after these things" (in the Hebrew Bible, both 22:1 and 22:20 begin, "And it happened after these things . . ."). Thus, given the story as we now have it, we can take the unit as 22:1–19, considering the possibility that 15–19 is an explanatory comment and seeing verse 20 as picking up the expression used in verse 1 to indicate a new beginning.

2. A second question to be asked in approaching a biblical story is: *what is the structure?* When the story was told, the teller could indicate the points of division with a pause, a change of his position, or a gesture, but since we have the story only in written form, we must try to detect the points where these pauses might have been made.

One way of getting at this is by trying to divide the story into scenes. Imagine that you are a director, assigned to staging the story for a dramatic production. You would have a series of scenes, along with some narrative transitional material between the scenes.

The first scene in this story would involve Abraham and God. We don't know where Abraham is. God is addressing him and Abraham is responding. This first scene includes verses 1 and 2. The point of the scene is the command given in verse 2. Note that there are actually three commands, with verbs in the imperative mood: "take . . . go . . . offer."

Verse 3 indicates how the command was carried out, using the same three words: "Took . . . offering . . . went . . . ," and serves as a transition to the next scene.

Scene two takes place somewhere along the way, a three-day journey from the starting place (vss. 4–8). The final scene is set on the mountain, with Abraham and his son present. Verses 9–14 tell what happens and 15–18 present a speech which the Lord makes. Verse 19 is a concluding narrative transition. In sum, the structure of the story looks like this:

> 1–2   Scene One: God's command to Abraham
> 3   Narrative transition. Abraham carries out the command
> 4–8   Scene Two: On the way to Moriah
>   4–5 Abraham, Isaac, and servants
>   6–8 Abraham and Isaac
> 9–18   Scene Three: On the mountain
>   9–14 Abraham, Isaac, the angel
>   15–18 Speech of the Lord
> 19   Narrative conclusion.

3. A third question to aid us in our listening is: *what are the devices of the storyteller?* We remember that the story was first told orally and thus we listen for techniques which a storyteller might use.

One such technique is *repetition* of words or phrases. These repetitions will help us to discover the major emphasis of the story. Note, for example, how many times the word "son" is repeated. Notice also that each time it occurs, it is accompanied by a pronoun which links son and father. In Hebrew this is always one word (like "myson" or "hisson"): "your son" (vs. 2), "his son" (vs. 6), "my son" (vs. 7), "my son" (vs. 8), "his son" (vs. 9), "your son" (vs. 12). The expression translated "your son, your only son" (literally, "your son, your only") is found in the first scene (vs. 2) and twice in the third scene (vss. 12, 16). The effect of the repetition of "son," always in relationship to the father, is to stress the preciousness of this son, the child of the promise (chap. 18) and the only one which Abraham and Sarah had.

Another example of repetition occurs with the words "take . . . go . . . offer." We have noted that these three commands are picked up in verse 3, which indicates how they are carried out. In verse 6, two of the verbs recur, as Abraham *took* the wood, *took* the fire and knife, and they *went*. The next time the verb "take" occurs is in verse 10, where Abraham *"took* the knife." In verse 13 all three verbs occur, "Abraham *went* and *took* the ram, and *offered* it. . . ." This ties up with the verbs of command in verse 2, but now the object of the taking and the offering is not the son but the ram. Thus the whole story revolves around God's command to "take, go, offer," Abraham's obeying, and God's surprising provision of that which is to be offered.

The link between these words at the beginning and end of the story point to another device of the storyteller: the *inclusio*. By this we mean the repetition of a word or phrase which serves to bracket a division of the story. Note how "so they went both of them together," brackets the section from verses 6–8. First there is silence as father and son walk along together. Then Isaac asks a question and his father gives an answer. Then again silence, as the two continue walking. The inclusio sets this section apart, encouraging us to reflect on it, to walk along with the father and son in our imagination, to think and to feel what they thought and felt.

We have noted that storytellers make use of *direct discourse*. This is the case with biblical storytellers, too. In this chapter we find direct discourse in verses 1, 2, 5, 7, 8, 11, 12, 16–18. (Jesus made great use of direct discourse in the stories he told. Note, for example, another father and son story in Luke 15:11–32. Direct discourse is found in verses 12, 17–19, 21–24, 27, 29–32). Direct discourse makes for more vivid storytelling. The story almost becomes a drama, with the teller taking the part of each of the characters in it.

Another interesting device is that of *varying the tempo* of the action. The storyteller can accelerate or decelerate time. Jacob Licht has spoken of the distinction between "telling time" and "action time."[3] For example, I can say, "Last summer, we drove from Minneapolis to Los Angeles." The action time for such was a number of days, but I can speed this up in the telling to just a few seconds. I can also slow down time when I am telling a story. For example:

> The count was three balls and two strikes. He watched the pitcher go into his wind-up. It was the last of the ninth inning, with two away. They were behind by two runs, and the bases were loaded. For an instant he remembered the hours, the months, the years, that had prepared him for this moment. He thought of his father pitching to him, every afternoon, in that little barnyard back home . . . and now, here he was, in the final game of the World Series . . .

The storyteller could spin out the story for several minutes, but the action time, from wind-up to delivery of the pitch, is only a matter of seconds.

Notice the way in which the tempo is varied in Genesis 22. The action described in verse 3 took place over a number of days; the telling time is only a

few seconds, but then note what happens in verse 9. The action is slowed
down, almost like a slow-motion instant replay, focusing on each detail:

> Abraham built an altar there,
> and laid the wood in order,
> and bound Isaac his son,
> and laid him on the altar, upon the wood.

Then in verse 10 the action slows down even more, so that telling time is just
about equal to action time,

> Then Abraham put forth his hand,
> and took the knife
> to slay his son.

For a good example of time acceleration, note Ruth 4:13. Here the action time
is more than nine months, while the telling time is only a matter of seconds.

Yet another device is *mimesis*, which means reproducing reality by imitat-
ing it. Professor Licht gives a good explanation:

> A small but vivid example of mimesis occurs in the story of Saul's first
> meeting with Samuel. He and his servant had been seeking the she-asses in
> vain; they decided to give up the search and to ask the 'seer' about them. Going
> up to the town where they hoped to find him they met some girls going down
> to fetch water. They asked them:
>
> "Is the seer here? and they answered them and said: He is! There
> before you! Quick now, because he has come to town today, because
> the people have a feast today at the high-place. As you come to town
> you will find him straight away, before he goes up to the high-place to
> eat, because the people won't eat till he comes, because he will bless
> the meal first, then will the guests eat. And now go up, because him,
> today you shall find him!" (1 Sam. 9, 11-13).
>
> The question is short, the answer could have been even shorter: "he is."
> (Biblical Hebrew has no word for 'yes'). It is, however, long and full of inter-
> esting though not quite relevant detail, and slightly disjointed in its grammar.
> It has been remarked that the girls talked so much because they enjoyed the
> company of a handsome stranger. The conclusion may be unwarranted, but the
> observation is correct. The girls are prattling—eager, excited and probably talk-
> ing all at once. We are not told that they prattled; their prattling is there on
> the page, caught from life and reproduced for the sheer joy of it.[4]

Biblical storytellers use other devices, too. Some are evident only in the
original language, such as alliteration (a series of words beginning with the
same letter, "tell a tale of terror") or assonance (similarity of sounds without

precise rhyme, such as "late, make"). We shall note some of these devices as
we listen to the stories.

Listen to those who are good storytellers. Try to discover some of their
techniques. Then watch, or better, listen for those techniques in the biblical
stories, remembering that they were told aloud before they were written
down.

4. We can distinguish between two settings for the biblical stories. The
first is the setting for the *action*: when and where did these happenings take
place? The second is the setting for the *composition*: when and where was this
account written down? These questions are often difficult to answer, and many
times they cannot be answered with certainty.

For example, in Genesis 22 the setting for the action is during the time of
the patriarchs. We cannot date this period precisely; the best we can do is to
say that the happenings recorded in Genesis 12–50 took place somewhere between the twentieth and seventeenth centuries B.C. Where did the action take
place? The location of Moriah is unknown. In 2 Chronicles 3:1, Mount Moriah
is located in Jerusalem. Visitors to that city will be shown the place where
Abraham was to sacrifice his son, but we do not know for certain. At the end
of the story Beersheba is mentioned. That city can be located, roughly fifty air-
miles south of Jerusalem.

What about the time and place for the composition of this story? We can
assume, first of all, that the story was told for generations among the members
of the family of Abraham. We suspect that in its earliest, oral form, it ended
with verse 14.

Then at some later date, the story was incorporated into the written collection of patriarchal materials (Gen. 12–50) and finally into the Priestly History
(Genesis through Numbers). This may have been a somewhat complex process, and scholars continue to debate just how it came about. For our purposes,
we can note that in its present setting in the book of Genesis, verses 15–18 tie
the Abraham-Isaac incident to the broader lines of the story of God's promise
to Abraham as given in Genesis 12.

When the Priestly History was given its final shaping in the sixth-century
exile, Genesis 22:1–19 was "frozen" in its present form and soon thereafter was
counted as part of those authoritative writings which the believing community
considered as Scripture.

5. Another question to ask is: what is the *intent* of the story? When a story
is told, the teller has some reason for telling it. If he is telling a joke, the intent

is to amuse. If he is spinning a yarn about the adventures of a great hero, the intent may be to entertain, but also to inspire.

The stories which we have in the Bible are often both amusing and entertaining; they may also inspire us, as we hear of the great figures from the history of Israel and the Christian church, but these stories have all been incorporated into the Bible. This means that those who passed them on and retold them always did so because they believed that these stories had something authoritative to say about God and people, about relationships between people, and about God, people, and the rest of creation. Thus we ought to ask of each story: what does this say about God? about God and people? about people and their relationships to one another? about God, people, and the whole of creation? In putting such questions to these stories, we are only dealing with them in a manner appropriate to the intent of the original tellers and writers.

To illustrate, once again, with our story from Genesis 22: the intent of this story has been understood in a number of ways. Some have said that it intends to say, "God does not want human sacrifices. Once and for all, this is now made clear." Others have suggested that its intent is to praise Abraham because of the great trust in God which he shows here. Elie Wiesel sees here the story of the suffering and sacrifice of the Jewish people.[5] Claus Westermann finds the clue to the meaning of the story in the suffering of the father. The story, he says, is addressed to those who have experienced such testings from God, such suffering. At the last moment, God delivers the son. For Abraham this does not mean, "I've passed the test," but rather, "My son is safe! Thank God!" Thus the story leads finally to the praise of God, and such is its intent.[6]

6. In hinting at these various understandings of the story in Genesis 22, we have suggested that a story may say different things to different times. How can we determine what a particular story has to say to us in our situation? One way of assisting in this process is to note some of the *new settings* which the old story is given, in the Bible itself as well as in the history of its interpretation.

The process of retelling the old stories begins in Scripture itself. This process might be compared to taking a diamond from an old ring and mounting it in a new setting. The new setting calls attention to facets of the original which were always there, but which had not been apparent in the original setting.

What new settings does the Bible provide for Genesis 22? The story is not retold in the Old Testament. A story like that of the Exodus from Egypt, for example, is retold, in a variety of ways, in such places as Deuteronomy 26,

Psalms 105 and 106, Hosea 11, and Nehemiah 9. The Genesis 22 incident is remembered in the Apocrypha. When old Mattathias speaks to his sons, encouraging them to be faithful to God despite the battles they were going to have to fight and the suffering they would experience, he reminds them of Abraham: "Was not Abraham found faithful when tested . . .?" (1 Mac. 2:52). In Sirach 44:19–22, Abraham's faithfulness under testing is remembered. Judith compares the testing of the Jews of her time to the testing which Abraham had to endure: "In spite of everything let us give thanks to the Lord our God, who is putting us to the test as he did our forefathers. Remember what he did with Abraham . . ." (Judith 8:25–26). Note that the hearers, the people, are to identify with Abraham. They are being tested, but they ought to give thanks to God nevertheless.

The process of picking up the story and giving it new settings continues in the New Testament. Hebrews 11:17–19 recalls the faith of Abraham. In James 2:18–26, Abraham is cited as an example to make the point that faith apart from works is dead. Romans 8:32 says, "He who did not spare his own Son but gave him up for us all. . . ." This may be an allusion to the Genesis 22 story; just as Abraham was ready to give up his son, so God had to give up his only Son, Jesus Christ. (Lectionary texts assigned for the first or the second Sundays in Lent, series B, link Genesis 22 with Romans 8:31–39.)

The process continues, both in the history of Judaism and of Christianity. Shalom Spiegel's book, *The Last Trial*, collects Jewish legends and retellings of the story. In his book, *Messengers of God*, Elie Wiesel calls this "a survivor's story" identifying himself with Isaac, the survivor. Søren Kirkegaard has written a classic essay on the story in *Fear and Trembling*. There are also new settings for the story in art (Rembrandt, Chagall) and music (Benjamin Britten, *War Requiem*). Each of these settings points to some new facet in the old story, as it is re-presented for a new time.

Our purpose in this chapter has not been to provide an interpretation of the story about Abraham and his only son, but rather to use this text to illustrate something of the way in which we can go about listening to the biblical stories. To summarize, we have said that while there is no method that one can rigidly apply to each biblical text, it is helpful to ask the following questions:

1. What is the unit?
2. What is the structure?
3. What are some of the devices of the storytellers?

4. What are the settings for the action and for the composition of the story?
5. What is the intent of the story?
6. What new settings has the story been given?

Keeping questions such as these in mind, we shall now get on with listening to some of the stories which the Bible tells.

CHAPTER 3

Matchmaker,
Matchmaker

Genesis 24

"Matchmaker, Matchmaker,
    Make me a match,
    Find me a find,
    Catch me a catch.
Matchmaker, Matchmaker,
    Look through your book
And make me a perfect match."[1]

The singer of these lines is Hodel, one of the five daughters of Tevye, the pious milkman in *Fiddler on the Roof*. Hodel expresses a concern as current as the latest Hollywood film and as ancient as the Bible: one young person hopes to meet another, to marry, and to make a "perfect match."

The Bible has a good deal to say about matchmaking. The book of Proverbs offers advice to young men about finding the right kind of woman for a wife. The Song of Solomon presents a collection of poetry celebrating the joys of love between a man and a woman, and Genesis tells a story about Abraham's son Isaac and the beautiful Rebekah.

Some Preliminaries

The story in Genesis 24 is a *unit* in itself. The "inclusio" device brackets the story, which begins with the order, "take a wife for my son Isaac" (vs. 4), and ends by saying that Isaac "took Rebekah, and she became his wife" (vs. 67). With 67 verses, this is the longest chapter in Genesis. It is almost as long as the whole book of Ruth (85 verses) and longer than the book of Jonah (48 verses).

If we could have heard this story as it was originally told, the teller would have paused at certain points, giving an indication of the *structure*. Imagining the story as a drama, we can divide it into four scenes, with transitional comments in between. Scene one involves Abraham and his servant (vss. 1–9). An inclusio brackets the scene, with the words "Put your hand under my thigh" at the beginning (vs. 2) and "So the servant put his hand under the thigh of Abraham . . ." at the end (vs. 9). Verse 10 is a transition, moving the servant to Mesopotamia. The second scene takes place at the city well. Those present are the servant and several women of the city, including Rebekah (vss. 11–27). Verses 28–31 provide the transition to scene three, at Rebekah's home (vss. 32–60). Verse 61 is a transition, getting Rebekah and her maids on the way, and leading into the final scene, where Isaac and Rebekah meet in the Negeb (vss. 62–67). Thus we have four main scenes: (1) Abraham and his servant at home (vss. 1–9); (2) the servant and Rebekah at the well (vss. 11–27); (3) the servant in Rebekah's home (vss. 32–60); (4) Isaac and Rebekah in the Negeb (vss. 62–67).

Before listening to the story, we can note some of the *devices of the storyteller*. Recalling the definition of a story as the narration of a sequence of events from a point of tension to a resolution of the tension, we see that the tension which drives this story is quite obvious. It is introduced in the order to "take a wife" (vs. 4). The whole story moves toward answering the question, "Who will be the wife for Isaac?" The tension is resolved only at the very end of the story when we are told that Isaac took Rebekah and she became his wife (vs. 67).

The storyteller makes much use of *direct discourse*. Some forty-four out of the sixty-seven verses are in direct speech, or roughly seventy percent of the story. This gives the teller a chance to dramatize and to make the account alive and vivid.

What about *repetitions*? The words "take a wife" (or variants) occur in verses 3, 4, 7, 37, 38, 40, and 67. The repeating of this phrase keeps the main theme of the story before us. But there is another phrase which occurs a number of times. Verse 21 says that "The man gazed at her in silence to learn whether the LORD had prospered his journey or not." The Hebrew expression is "prosper his way." That same expression occurs in verse 40, "The LORD, before whom I walk, will send his angel with you and prosper your way," where the servant reports what Abraham had told him, and also in verse 42 where he repeats his prayer, ". . . if now thou wilt prosper the way which I go." In verse 56, the servant says to Rebekah's family, "Do not delay me, since the LORD has prospered my way." Verse 40 indicates that "send his angel with you" is related to that phrase; the same thought is expressed in verse 7 when Abraham says, "he will send his angel before you." Then, in verse 27 the servant says, "the LORD has led me in the way" and in verse 48, "who had led me by the right way." All of these expressions have to do with God's guidance of the servant, a guidance assured by Abraham in the promise about the angel (vs. 7), reflected upon by the servant as he sat by the well (vs. 21), and then affirmed after he had discovered who Rebekah was (vs. 27) and had met her family (vs. 56).

These repetitions give us the clue to the twin themes of this story. First, there is the theme about finding a wife for Isaac. But along with this is the "prosper the journey" theme and the language about the angel, which indicates that the story also intends to say something about God's guidance.

Note how the storyteller *varies the tempo* as he tells the story. Verse 10 is a good example of time acceleration, telling in a matter of seconds about events which took many days. The transition in verses 28–31 also accelerates the action, quickly getting Rebekah home, where she tells the story of what had happened (vs. 28) and then getting Laban back to the well. Not only is the action compressed, but the verb "ran" is used twice, giving the whole transition a sense of urgency and breathless excitement. At the beginning of the third scene, verses 32–33 accelerate the action, telling of getting to the house, ungirding the camels, feeding them, washing up, and setting the table, all in a few words which would take only seconds of telling time. After the long speech of the servant (vss. 34–49), where telling time and action time are just about equal, the evening's eating, drinking, and sleeping are compressed into a few words (vs. 54). The transitional verse 61 accelerates the tempo. Finally, the whole process of the wedding and the beginning of married life is compressed into, "Isaac brought her into the tent, and took Rebekah, and she became his wife; and he loved her" (vs. 67).

Think of hearing this story, with your imagination furnishing the video component. You listen to Abraham's solemn speech to his trusted servant. Then suddenly the servant and all of the camels are whisked to Mesopotamia. There the tempo slows down as you imagine the scene at the well. Along with the servant, you observe every movement of the beautiful Rebekah. Can she be the one for Isaac? Then the tempo speeds up as you are taken to her home. You listen carefully to the servant's speech, the debating of the family, and then you follow Rebekah as she starts out on her journey. Finally, you watch Isaac as he goes out for a walk in the evening, notices camels in the distance, meets Rebekah, and takes her as his wife. Imagine the storyteller varying the speed of his telling, dramatizing the speeches of the characters, pausing, and making effective use of silence (after verse 21, for example). In such a way you can begin to get an idea of the dramatic impact of this ancient account.

What of the *setting for the action* of this story? We are not told where Abraham and his servant are at the beginning; we could assume Hebron, since that was the setting for the events of the previous chapter. Scene two takes place in the "city of Nahor" which appears to mean Haran, in northern Mesopotamia, where Abraham's grandfather Nahor had lived. The last scene takes place in the Negeb, the sourthern part of the land of Canaan. As for the time when the events take place, we can do no better than speak in broad terms of the patriarchal period, somewhere between the twentieth and seventeenth centuries B.C.

What about the *setting for the composition* of the story? We assume, once again, that an early version of this story was told and retold in the family of Abraham and his descendants for generations. There are two other biblical stories which are somewhat similar to this one: the account of Jacob and Rachel in Genesis 29 and that of Moses finding his wife in Exodus 2:15–22. All three stories take place at a well, and all three end up with a marriage. But in comparing the three, it is apparent that the story in Genesis 24 is the most carefully constructed. Who was the writer who put the story into the form in which it now stands? While the matter is debated, there is good reason to believe that he worked during the time of King Solomon. Because he used the name "Yahweh" or "Jahwe" for God, he is identified as the "J" writer. This was the age of "Solomon and all his glory." Israel was a powerful nation, with international contacts and interests. Wisdom literature, such as we find in the book of Proverbs, and similar to that which is found in Egypt and Mesopotamia, flourished during this period. The Bible reader will recall that the major concerns of Proverbs are not with heavenly things, but with secular, down-to-earth matters. The mood of this story, as well as that of the Joseph story and the story of Ruth, reflects this secular orientation. We do not hear of angels intervening at the last moment (Gen. 22) or of God entering the sequence of ordinary events through angelic messengers who can perform miracles (Judg. 6, 13). Everything takes place in an everyday, matter-of-fact way, but God is nevertheless present and active. Here is a writer who speaks about God in non-religious language.

We can classify this story as a "family story" since its concern has to do with finding a wife, an event which takes place within the sphere of the family. The *intent* of a family story is to deal with matters of birth, marriage, death, and relationships within a family. However, we have already seen that the story has another theme: that of God's guidance. We suggest that here we have a family story, carefully reshaped into a guidance story, the intent of which is to indicate something of the way in which God is active in the ordinary events of everyday life.

The Story

Because the translation is so clear and crisp, we shall now follow the *Good News Bible* (GNB) as we turn to the story in Genesis 24.

1. We have seen that the first scene begins with the expression, "Place your hand between my thighs" (vs. 2) and concludes with, "So the servant put his hand between the thighs of Abraham, his master, and made a vow to do what Abraham had asked" (vs. 9). The exact nature of this act is no longer clear to us, but it was apparently a way of making a very solemn promise, involving contact with the source of the seed for the next generation. Abraham's order to his servant is first a negative one:

> "I want you to make a vow in the name of the LORD, the God of heaven and earth, that you will not choose a wife for my son from the people here in Canaan." (Gen. 24:3, GNB)

Why should Isaac not marry a Canaanite woman? Abraham's objection to such a mixed marriage was a religious one. The matter is put clearly in Deuteronomy 7:3–4 which says, speaking about the peoples living in Canaan where the Israelites would settle:

> "Do not marry any of them, and do not let your children marry any of them, because then they would lead your children away from the LORD to worship other gods." (GNB)

The second part of Abraham's order is positive,

"You must go back to the country where I was born and get a wife for my son Isaac from among my relatives." (Gen. 24:4, GNB)

Like an immigrant family in the days of the settling of the midwestern United States, the father said, "Go back to the old country and find a nice Norwegian (or Dutch, or Irish) girl for our son to marry!"

There is another part to Abraham's order to his servant. He says, "But you must not under any circumstances take my son back there" (vs. 8, GNB). Why was this? Isaac might go back to the "old country" and like it so well that he would decide to stay there! But Abraham knew that the Lord had brought him and his family to this new land, and had promised that one day it would belong to him and his descendants. Abraham had lived by that promise ever since, and he expected his son to do the same.

There are two matters of special theological interest in this first scene. First is the divine name, "the LORD, the God of heaven and earth" (vs. 3, GNB; cf. vs. 7). This expression occurs only here in the patriarchal narratives. As we hear it, we are reminded of the first verse of the Bible, "In the beginning God created the heavens and the earth." The Lord is here described not as the God of Abraham and his family, but as *the* God of all that exists. Here is a some-what amazing aspect of the biblical faith. The God who has created heaven and earth and all that exists also cares about what happens in the lives of two young people. The God of heaven and earth is also a God who cares about matchmaking.

Also of interest is the comment in verse 7, "he will send his angel before you." The Bible tells of God's angel leading the nation through the wilderness (Exod. 23:20; 32:34). God also sends his angel to protect the individual (Ps. 91:11). In the story of Tobit, an ordinary man appears who accompanies To-bias on his journey; it turns out that this man is actually an angel (Tobit 5). Watch for the angel in the story of Isaac and Rebekah. When does the angel appear, and what does he do?

The storyteller is not interested in saying anything about the journey to Mesopotamia. Accelerating time, he says, "The servant, who was in charge of Abraham's property, took ten of his master's camels and went to the city where Nahor had lived in northern Mesopotamia" (vs. 10, GNB). Thus we are pre-pared for the next scene, at the city well.

2. In the towns of Israel, the men gathered at the gate (Gen. 23:10) and the women at the well. We can imagine the daily routine, picking up the water jug, walking down to the well, greeting friends, exchanging a bit of

gossip, and then walking back home. On this particular occasion there was a stranger at the well, a stranger accompanied by ten camels!

> When he arrived, he made the camels kneel down at the well outside the city. It was late afternoon, the time when women came out to get water. He prayed, "LORD, God of my master Abraham, give me success today and keep your promise to my master. Here I am at the well where the young women of the city will be coming to get water. I will say to one of them, 'Please, lower your jar and let me have a drink.' If she says, 'Drink, and I will also bring water for your camels,' may she be the one that you have chosen for your servant Isaac." (vss. 11–14, GNB)

This part of the story tells us something about prayer. The Bible contains a collection of prayers, designed to be used in formal worship services. These are found in the book of Psalms, the prayerbook and the hymnbook of ancient Israel and of the church. But the Bible also gives examples of prayers that arise quite spontaneously in the midst of a situation in everyday life. Such is the prayer that we have here. Both the formal and the free spontaneous prayer have always had their place in the life of the people of god. Now, for the first time, we meet Rebekah:

> Before he had finished praying, Rebecca arrived with a water jar on her shoulder. She was the daughter of Bethuel, who was the son of Abraham's brother Nahor and his wife Milcah. She was a very beautiful young girl and still a virgin. She went down to the well, filled her jar, and came back. The servant ran to meet her and said, "Please give me a drink of water from your jar." (vss. 15–17, GNB)

Here we learn that Rebekah is of the right family. She is the daughter of Abraham's nephew, Bethuel. We also learn that she is very beautiful, young, and a virgin. The servant, at this point in the story, does not know who she is. He asks his question, and a tension is introduced: will she offer to water his camels? will she be the answer to his prayer?

Now the storyteller speeds up the action. The young woman says, "Drink, sir," and *quickly* lowers her jar. She offers to get water for the camels, and *quickly* empties her jar into the trough and then *runs* to the well to get more water, until all ten camels have had their fill—a task, one suspects, which took considerable time and energy!

In contrast to the young woman's activity, the servant "kept watching her in silence, to see if the LORD had given him success" (vs. 21, GNB). What does he know about this young woman? She is beautiful, kindhearted, and cares about animals. We might also add that she has a sturdy constitution, to make all those trips with the water jug! But is she the answer to prayer? Is she the right one? He gets no direct word from God. No voice from heaven says, "She is the one!" He must take a risk and make a decision. So he asks, first of all, about her family, "Please tell me who your father is" (vs. 23, GNB). When he discovers that she is from his master's clan, he can only say, "Praise the LORD, the God of my master Abraham, who has faithfully kept his promise to my master. The LORD has led me straight to my master's relatives" (vs. 27, GNB).

Now again, the storyteller speeds up the action. The young woman runs home, tells about what has happened, and then Laban runs back, all in the space of two sentences (vss. 28–29). Laban has noticed the ring and the bracelets that his sister has received from the stranger. He is quite willing to welcome this apparently wealthy emissary from the new world as a guest, and insists that he (and his ten camels) stay overnight.

3. When the guest arrives at Rebekah's home, he discovers that the table has been set and the meal is ready (vs. 33). But the meal does not begin until some time later (vs. 54). The servant has a job to do, and he wants to get at it immediately. So he explains the nature of his mission:

> "I am the servant of Abraham," he began. "The LORD has greatly blessed my master and made him a rich man. He has given him flocks of sheep and goats, cattle, silver, gold, male and female slaves, camels, and donkeys. Sarah, my master's wife, bore him a son when she was old, and my master has given everything he owns to him." (vss. 34–36, GNB)

At first reading, the servant's lengthy speech may seem a needless and boring repetition of what has already been told, but if we listen to this speech carefully, we discover that it fits the occasion, and provides some new insights. For example, the story began with the assertion about Abraham, "and the LORD had blessed him in everything he did" (vs. 1). In his speech to Rebekah's family, the servant expands upon this theme. These people had not heard from Abraham for a time, and he makes explicit what it means to be blessed by the Lord. Here "blessing" means possessions, a good life, and the gift of offspring.

The Bible speaks of two fundamental shapes of God's activity with his people. God has delivered them from bondage. In the Old Testament, the story of the deliverance from Egypt is the chief example of God's delivering activity. The New Testament centers on the deliverance from the bondage of sin, death, and the power of the devil, which was brought about on the cross of Jesus Christ. But the Bible also speaks of another way in which God works. This is not a single, dramatic act, but an ongoing, continuous action, such as the giving of sunshine and rain, health and strength, family and friends, and all of the commonplace gifts which make life possible. The Bible calls this activity blessing. In the introduction to the servant's speech we learn something about blessing. The servant acknowledges that all that Abraham had was a gift of the Lord, including the son born to him in his old age.[2]

The servant's speech also helps us to understand Abraham's promise, "He will send his angel before you . . ." (vs. 7, GNB). In his retelling of the promise, the servant says, "[He] will send his angel with you and give you success" (vs. 40, GNB; [RSV, "and prosper your way"]). Now we understand what "sending his angel" means. God will cause what the servant does to succeed. No angel, in the form of a human being or a heavenly creature, ever spoke to the servant. But God's angel, unseen, unheard, was present nevertheless, directing the servant's footsteps and giving him a successful mission.

The servant reviews what had happened at the well and then comes to the point, asking for Rebekah as Isaac's wife. He continues:

> "Now, if you intend to fulfill your responsibility toward my master and treat him fairly, please tell me; if not, say so, and I will decide what to do." (vs. 49, GNB)

When this good and pious family hears this story from this visitor from the new land, they can only say,

> "Since this matter comes from the LORD, it is not for us to make a decision. Here is Rebecca; take her and go. Let her become the wife of your master's son, as the LORD himself has said." (vss. 50–51, GNB)

The servant gives thanks to the Lord, distributes some gifts to the family, and then the meal begins.

The next morning the servant, with admirable singleness of purpose, wants to get on with things. His mission has been accomplished, and he is ready to set out with Rebekah. But the family doesn't want to rush matters:

> But Rebecca's brother and her mother said, "Let the girl stay with us a week or ten days, and then she may go."
> But he said, "Don't make us stay. The LORD has made my journey a success; let me go back to my master." (vss. 55–56, GNB)

Finally someone suggests, "Let's call the girl and find out what she has to say" (vs. 57, GNB). Just the day before, Rebekah had picked up her waterpot and set out for the well. Now, just twenty-four hours later, they were talking about her picking up everything she owned and setting out to meet her husband! Indeed, someone should ask how she felt about all this!

> So they called Rebecca and asked, "Do you want to go with this man?" (vs. 58, GNB)

The Hebrew text gives her answer in one word: "['ēlēk] I will go" (vs. 58).

And that decides it. Rebekah will go. Her "match" has been made. Her family gives her a blessing as she departs, wishing for her many descendants and for these descendants political success. (We suspect that here we see a concern of the writer, during Israel's heyday in the time of Solomon.) They start out on their way toward the land of Canaan.

4. To this point, we have heard nothing of Isaac. In the final scene of the story, we are to imagine him at home, taking a walk in the cool of the evening.

The biblical storyteller describes the meeting of Isaac and Rebekah with skill and even a romantic touch. We translate the Hebrew literally: Isaac is out in the field,

> and he lifted up his eyes and looked,
> and behold, camels were coming!
> And Rebekah lifted up her eyes
> and she saw Isaac . . . (vss. 63–64)

Their eyes meet, and then they meet, and the servant tells the story of all that has happened. Then, rapidly accelerating the sequence of events, the storyteller informs us that Isaac brought Rebekah into the tent, she became his wife, and he loved her.

Thus the chain of events which began with Abraham saying, "get a wife for my son" now ends, as the young couple begin their new life together.

For a New Time

The story about Isaac and Rebekah has been told one more time. Think of the times and places it has been told. It started with the servant. He told the story about what had happened at the well to the family of Rebekah. Then he told the story again to Isaac, when they met in the Negeb. The story would have stayed in the family. We can imagine young Jacob asking his parents, "How did you ever meet?" Perhaps Rebekah began by saying, "One evening I said to my family, 'I think I'll go down to the well.' " Or maybe Isaac would say, "One evening I said to my servant, 'I think I'll go out for a walk.' "

How would they have told the story? They would have told about the servant, the camels, and the first time they saw each other. And they would have said something about the Lord working in their lives, though they were not aware of that at the time. The story remained in the family and then, long after, when materials were being collected for an account of the whole story of God and God's people, this love story was included in that collection. From that time on it would be read, told, and retold, in Hebrew families, Jewish families, Christian families, and the telling goes on to this day.

What was the point of the telling? As a family story, this account told how Isaac got his wife. All of us continue to tell such stories in our own families. At the right time, a father or mother will say to listening children, "Now let me tell you how we first met . . . ," and the tale begins to spin.

The family story of Rebekah and Isaac has something more to say. It says something about God and people, as it tells about angels, prayer, and matchmaking.

1. We have called attention to Abraham's assuring word, "He will send his angel before you" and have asked that you watch for the angel in the story. But the angel never appears.

This is quite different from other stories about angels in the Bible. We can recall a trio of strangers, calling on Abraham and Sarah. Only later were they recognized as angels (Gen. 18; see Heb. 13:2). We shall hear about an ordinary appearing person who converses with Gideon (Judg. 6) and another who speaks with the parents of Samson (Judg. 13); when they performed wondrous acts, it became apparent that they were angels. We have already noted how the voice of an angel spoke to Abraham at the last second telling him not to sacrifice his son Isaac (Gen. 22).

In this story the angel never appears, nor does the angel speak. What does the story mean, in speaking about the angel?

We have noted the importance of the guidance theme in this chapter. The RSV translated this theme in terms of God "prospering the way" of the servant; the GNB translated it as "giving success." The clue to what is meant by the angel occurs in verse 40. The servant quotes his master Abraham as saying, "The LORD, whom I have always obeyed, will send his angel with you and give you success" (GNB; the RSV says, "and prosper your way"). The two expressions mean the same thing. For God to send his angel along with someone means that God will prosper that person's way and give success. This is a way of speaking about God's care: "The LORD will send his angel with you." The same way of speaking occurs at the conclusion of both the morning and evening prayers which Martin Luther composed for family use: "Let thy holy angel have charge concerning me, that the wicked one have no power over me."

In his book, *God's Angels Need No Wings*, Claus Westermann puts it this way: "It is the intention of the Bible not to provide a special figure apart from and in addition to God but rather to emphasize God's care for what is endangered and unprotected in particular proximity to a person. This care of God can best be understood by talking about an angel."[3]

2. This story also has something to say about prayer. We have noted that the Bible contains a collection of formal prayers, in the words of praise and lament gathered together in the book of Psalms. But this story exemplifies another kind of prayer, which reacts to a concrete situation and is concerned with a specific need. Both types of prayer are proper for God's people, and the one enriches the other. The free, spontaneous prayer can invigorate fixed prayers which are in danger of becoming stilted and formalized. Formal, liturgical prayers can act as a check against too much repetition and since they are older and time-tested, they can teach us how to pray. In the Christian tradition we use the Lord's Prayer, the Psalms, and certain liturgical prayers in our worship. But this story reminds us that we are also called to "pray without ceasing" and that the spontaneous prayer in reaction to a specific situation is also a mark of the lifestyle of the people of God.

How was the servant's prayer answered? Not in any dramatic, spectacular manner. The servant heard no voice saying, "She's the one!" The answer came in the actions and words of a young woman, who offered water to a weary traveler and his camels. The servant had to reflect on these actions, and then make a decision that involved a risk: she must be the one!

This story encourages us to pray, then to risk action, believing that the God who hears everyday prayers answers them in everyday ways, through the caring words and acts of other people.

3. Finally, what of the matchmaking theme?

We have seen that when this story speaks about God, it speaks of the "God of heaven and earth." The God of Abraham is the God of Genesis 1, who created and sustains all that exists in the entire universe.

But as the story unfolds, we discover that this God is also concerned about the lives of two ordinary people. In order for the story of Abraham and his descendants to continue, it is necessary that a child be born (Gen. 15, 16, 18). It is also necessary that two people meet and fall in love. This love story also belongs to the story of God and God's people.

We shall discover that the story of Ruth also indicates that God is concerned with people in their meeting and marrying. One of the wisdom writers, in a collection which could well have been assembled when Genesis 24 was being put into its present form, expressed it this way:

> House and wealth are inherited from fathers,
>   but a prudent wife is from the LORD. (Prov. 19:14)

According to this story, the Maker of heaven and earth cares about matchmaking, too.

CHAPTER 4

God Is Working His Purpose Out

(PURPOSE Irregular)

Genesis 37—50

Several years ago while paging through *The New Yorker*, I came across this bit of filler at the bottom of the page:

GOD IS WORKING HIS PURPOSE OUT
  PURPOSE Irregular

—The Worshipbook, a Presbyterian
hymnal published by the
Westminster Press

How true.[1]

The "How true" after the item represented the editor's comment on the hymn title and the indication of tune and meter. It has seemed to me that this hymn title, along with the indication of tune, meter, *and* the editorial comment, captures very well what the Joseph story has to say.

Some Preliminaries

Chapters 37–50 of Genesis are concerned with Joseph, making this the longest of the narratives in Genesis. The story begins with Joseph at the age of seventeen (37:2), continues with the account of his activities as special assistant to the Pharaoh at thirty (41:46), and concludes with a report of his death at the age of one hundred and ten years (50:26).

While Joseph is mentioned at the beginning and end of this lengthy section, there are two chapters which separate themselves from the Joseph story. Chapter 38 tells about Judah and Tamar. Chapter 49 collects the blessings which Jacob pronounces upon each of his twelve sons. In fact, the tension which is introduced in chapter 37, the conflict between Joseph and his brothers, is resolved in chapter 45. Then the broad *structure* of the Joseph story looks like this:

    I   Joseph and his brothers: shalom shattered (37)

    II Judah and Tamar (38)

    III Joseph in Egypt: success (39–41)

    IV Joseph and his brothers: shalom restored (42–45)

    V Jacob's family comes to Egypt (46–50)

Thus the major parts of the Joseph story proper are I, III, and IV of the above outline.

The beginning of the story indicates the type of material or *genre* of that which follows: "and this is the story of Jacob's family" (37:2, GNB). This is, first of all, a family story. We might observe that this is a very realistic family story which tells it like it is, not as it ought to be. Sometimes we have sentimental notions about brotherly love in the Bible, and idealized images of these patriarchal homes, but here we see a family which is torn apart by rivalry and stress. We hear about a father with a favorite son, brothers who are envious, jealousy which comes close to attempted murder. We learn about another family member, Judah, who forgets a promise made to a widow, and who consorts with a woman he believes to be a prostitute. Millions of people in our time follow the modern equivalent of the family story, the "soap opera," on television each day. These programs are popular because they, too, tell it like it is in families, though one hopes that the picture they present is an exaggerated one! But the themes of childlessness and childbearing, jealousy and sibling rivalry, favoritism and infidelity, are common to both the daily television series and the narratives in Genesis 12–50.

The Joseph story is a family story, but as the Bible presents it to us, it is more than that. Two passages provide us with a clue to the *intent* of the story in its present form. In 45:7–8 we recognize some of the same language which we heard in Genesis 24, as Joseph addresses his brothers: "God sent me ahead of you to rescue you in this amazing way and to make sure that you and your descendants survive. So it was not really you who sent me here, but God" (GNB, cf. 24:7). And in the last chapter, "As for you, you meant evil against me; but God meant it for good, to bring it about that many people should be kept alive, as they are today" (50:20). Both passages make clear the writer's conviction that God was working through all of the events which took place to accomplish God's purpose (even though those purposes must have seemed most "irregular" on many an occasion!). It would appear that in these two passages we have a comment from the one who finally shaped the story. Thus we have here a family story, told and retold for decades and centuries, but then reshaped into a guidance story, telling how God leads and guides the lives of individuals and of communities.

The *tension* which drives this story is introduced at the very beginning: "When his brothers saw that their father loved Joseph more than he loved them, they hated their brother so much that they would not speak to him in a friendly manner" (37:4, GNB). The word "shalom" occurs here in the Hebrew text: the idea is that the brothers could not speak peaceably to Joseph (RSV) or that they could not give him the customary greeting, "Shalom!" In 45:15, after Joseph has revealed himself to his brothers, "his brothers spoke with him" (author's translation). Finally, after the death of their father, the Hebrew text says of Joseph that "he spoke to their hearts" (50:21), that is, he comforted them. The brothers wouldn't speak to Joseph; they spoke with him; he spoke to "their hearts." Such is the movement of the story, as the tension introduced at the beginning is finally resolved.

The *setting for the action* of the story is at first in the land of Canaan. From chapter 39 on, the action takes place in Egypt. This is the first time in the biblical story that the descendants of Abraham encounter a great world empire. There is in the story something of the fascination that a newcomer from a rural society would feel when visiting the capital city of a strange land. Thus we find the story noting the trappings of leadership: the signet ring, the fine garments, the gold chain, the royal chariot, and the cry of the people as a high government official rides along the streets (41:42–43). We detect an interest in the foreign language, with the note about Joseph's Egyptian name (41:45), and the description of the interpreter needed to facilitate business with people from other lands (42:23). There are comments about the religion of these people; Joseph himself has married into a clergy family (41:45) and engages in the practice of divination (44:5). Joseph lives to be 110 years, the ideal age, according to the Egyptian view; an Egyptian text, "The Instruction of the Vizier Ptah-Hotep," says, "I attained one hundred and ten years of life which the king gave me."[2] Finally, after Joseph's death, he is embalmed and put in a coffin in the Egyptian manner (50:26).

When was it that an Israelite went to Egypt and attained such a high position in the government? Unfortunately, the Bible identifies neither the Pharaoh with whom Joseph worked nor the new Pharaoh "who did not know Joseph" (Exod. 1:8). Some have identified the Pharaoh under whom Joseph worked as one of the Hyksos rulers, foreigners who controlled Egypt for about a hundred years, from 1650–1542 B.C.[3] For our purposes, it is enough to note that in the Joseph story we have a biblical account which tells how it happened that some of the descendants of Jacob, also named Israel, went down to Egypt, later to become slaves.

What do we know of the *compositional setting* for the story? Biblical critics have traditionally divided it up among the sources J, E, and P, thus assuming a composition from the time of Solomon (the J material) down to the exile (the P material). However, there has been no agreement on the source analysis of these chapters, and the tendency in recent scholarship has been to view the Joseph story as a unity.[4] It would seem reasonable to assume that the story about Joseph was often told among those Israelites who settled in Egypt. The story then circulated among the different tribes, with some differences in emphasis. Remnants of two major versions (labeled J and E) can be detected in Genesis 37–50 but cannot be separated with certainty. The story as we now have it was most likely written down during the time of King Solomon, probably by the J writer. As was the case with other biblical materials, it was updated and annotated in subsequent retellings. Finally, during the time of the exile in Babylon (587–539 B.C.) it was "frozen" into its final form.

Another feature which links the Joseph story to the time of Solomon is the similarity which it has to material from the book of Proverbs, that is with wisdom material. Gerhard von Rad has argued that this is a "didactic wisdom story," coming from the same circles which collected the material which we now find in the book of Proverbs.[5] While von Rad's thesis has been contested, its main lines are convincing. In other words, both the material in Proverbs and the Joseph story are teaching the same thing, but the form of the instruction is different. Proverbs teaches by means of short sayings, while the Joseph story teaches by means of a story. Joseph himself exemplifies the virtues which we find advocated in Proverbs. Speaking of the wisdom writers, von Rad says:

> They depict a man who by his upbringing, his modesty, his learning, his courtesy and his self-discipline has acquired true nobility of character. He is, let us say it at once, the image of Joseph! Joseph, as the writer of the narrative draws him, is the very picture of just such a young man at his best, well-bred and finely educated, steadfast in faith and versed in the ways of the world.[6]

A few examples: Genesis 39 teaches by means of narrative what Proverbs 22:14 and 23:27–28 teach through sayings. Joseph has extraordinary control over his emotions (Gen. 42:24; 43:30f.; 45:1 indicates the stress he felt); cf. Proverbs 17:27; 15:18; 16:32. Joseph is not eager for revenge; cf. Proverbs 24:29 and 10:12. We have noted the texts which speak of God's guidance, in Genesis 45 and 50; cf. Proverbs 16:9, "A man's mind plans his way, but the LORD directs his steps," and also Proverbs 19:21, "Many are the plans in the mind of a man, but it is the purpose of the LORD that will be established." The mysterious relationship between human action and divine guidance is also expressed in Proverbs 20:24, "A man's steps are ordered by the LORD; how then can man understand his way?"

In sum, it seems most likely that the Joseph story in essentially its present form is a product of the time of Solomon. This was a period of international contact, of exchange with Egypt, and of a general interest in things foreign. The author took up traditional materials about Joseph and shaped them into a narrative which addressed his own time, and which reflects the spirit of that time. We have already noted that this was a secular age which was reluctant to speak about angels intervening in the historical process or about charismatic leaders endowed with special gifts. The tone of wisdom literature, such as Proverbs, is sober, realistic, down-to-earth. Its concern is not with the next world, but with how to get along in this one. Such is the atmosphere of Solomonic wisdom, and such is the spirit of the Joseph story, too.

Joseph and His Brothers: Shalom Shattered (Genesis 37)

The story begins by telling us that Joseph was seventeen years old. This in itself gives us a clue to the intended audience. The instructional material in Proverbs is directed to young men, who will some day attain positions of leadership. This story is aimed at the same audience. Whoever is seventeen (or can remember being seventeen) can immediately identify with the main character. Here, the story also tells us that with his brothers, Joseph took care of sheep and goats. But then we hear the note, "He brought bad reports to his father about what his brothers were doing" (37:2, GNB). Since no one loves a tattler, it is clear from the start that there will be trouble between Joseph and his eleven brothers.

The story continues with another cause for friction. Joseph was the son of his father's old age. As we review the biblical story, we discover that Jacob fathered ten sons and a daughter (Gen. 29:31–30:20) before Rachel, his beloved, was able to conceive. We remember that "Rachel was shapely and beautiful. . . . Jacob worked seven years so that he could have Rachel, and the time seemed like only a few days to him, because he loved her" (Gen. 29:17, 20, GNB). For a long time Rachel had no children. But then, when Jacob was getting on in years, she gave birth to Joseph. Some time later Benjamin was born, and Rachel died at that birth (Gen. 35:18–20). The biblical story simply reports, "Jacob loved Joseph more than all his other sons, because he had been born to him when he was old" (37:3, GNB). Joseph was his father's favorite. Such things can happen in families! This favor expresses itself in an act: Jacob gave Joseph a beautiful new jacket, with long sleeves. We can imagine the younger brother, who already had a reputation as a tattler, wearing it in front of his brothers. This increased the tension between them all the more, and the brothers wouldn't greet Joseph with "Shalom" when they met.

There is yet another cause for the brothers to be angry with Joseph. He had dreamed, and he had to tell his brothers about his dream. With a literal translation of the Hebrew, we catch the excitement as Joseph told it:

> And look—we were binding sheaves in the middle of the field,
> and look—my bundle got up and stood up,
> and look—your bundles gathered around mine, and bowed down to my
> bundle. (37:7)

Then Joseph, who did not know enough to quit, told another dream. Once again, translating the Hebrew literally:

> Look—I dreamed another dream,
> and look—the sun and the moon and eleven stars all were bowing down to
> me. (37:9)

So the tension in the story is introduced and intensified. Joseph the tattler,

Joseph the favorite son, Joseph the one with the arrogant dreams. His brothers become jealous and hate him. His father scolds him but keeps those strange dreams in mind (and so do we who hear the story). He must have wondered, "What will become of this boy?" The Christian reader cannot but think of a young Jewish mother who had the same question, and who "kept all these things, pondering them in her heart" (Luke 2:19).

Then one day Joseph's father sends him to check on his brothers, who are taking care of sheep near Shechem, several days journey from their home in Hebron. Away from his father, Joseph seems helpless. He immediately gets lost (37:15). Then we listen in on the conversation of the brothers, as they see Joseph, with his new jacket, in the distance:

> "Here comes that dreamer. Come on now, let's kill him and throw his body into one of the dry wells. We can say that a wild animal killed him. Then we will see what becomes of his dreams." (37:19–20, GNB)

The coat. The dreams. Those were the things that bothered the brothers. So they ripped off the coat and threw the dreamer into an empty well.

The final scene in this chapter takes place back home in Hebron. Jacob is shown his son's new jacket, now stained with blood. The brothers say, "We found this. Does it belong to your son?" (37:32). (He is not "our brother!") Jacob does recognize it and draws the logical inference, "Yes, it is his! Some wild animal has killed him. My son Joseph has been torn to pieces!" (37:33, GNB).

All his sons and daughters try to comfort the old man, but it is no use. The favorite son is gone. The dreamer, Jacob believes, is dead. The brothers know that he's been taken away as a slave. But we who hear the story know what has really happened to Joseph. He has been taken to Egypt, and is now working for one of the officers of Pharaoh.

Joseph in Egypt: Success (Genesis 39–41)

We have noted that one of the devices of the biblical storytellers is repetition of a key word or theme. After the interlude concerning the affair between Judah and Tamar (Gen. 38), the story picks up with Joseph working for Potiphar in Egypt. Four times the expression, "The LORD was with Joseph" occurs (39:2, 3, 21, 23). In three of these cases it is linked with a declaration about Joseph's success (vss. 2, 3, 23). We are also told that, "because of Joseph the LORD blessed the household of the Egyptian and everything that he had in his

house and in his fields" (39:5, GNB). This talk of "success" and "the LORD was
with Joseph" is the language of blessing. Here we see a good example of what
is meant by blessing: the quiet, unnoticed, ongoing action of God; the granting of success, fertility, good things in everyday life. The biblical reader is reminded of the promise to Abraham, "so that you will be a blessing," in Genesis 12:2. So Joseph is successful and has been put in charge of Potiphar's household and of all he owns.

But then there is the matter of Potiphar's wife. Wealthy, bored, with time
on her hands, she has noticed this handsome new employee:

> Joseph was well-built and good-looking, and after a while his master's wife
> began to desire Joseph and asked him to go to bed with her. He refused and
> said, to her, "Look, my master does not have to concern himself with anything
> in the house, because I am here. He has put me in charge of everything he
> has. . . . How then could I do such an immoral thing and sin against God?"
> Although she asked Joseph day after day, he would not go to bed with her.
> (39:6–10, GNB)

One afternoon, however, she catches Joseph by his jacket and tries to force his
affections. He runs out, leaving her with the jacket in her hands. Humiliated,
she calls to the other servants:

> "Look at this! This Hebrew that my husband brought to the house is insulting
> us. He came into my room and tried to rape me, but I screamed as loud as I
> could. When he heard me scream, he ran outside, leaving his robe beside me."
> (39:14–15, GNB)

Once again, Joseph's jacket provides the evidence from which an inference is
drawn. She shows it to her husband, putting the blame for the whole matter
on him: "That Hebrew slave that you brought here . . ." (39:17, GNB). Then
Joseph, who has resisted temptation and done the right thing, is thrown into
prison. Claus Westermann comments:

> This God, however, immediately after his expression of trust brings him into
> prison! The narrator intends to say through this that God really is like this. He
> does not allow his deeds to be calculated by men, even by his own. He is not
> the dear God of pious history where everything always goes right. . . . It is
> possible that a decision made in obedience to God can bring a man directly into
> catastrophe.[7]

Joseph did the right thing, and ended up in prison. There, too, the Lord is with
him, and he is soon put in charge of the other prisoners.

Some time later, Pharaoh's wine steward and his baker are put into the same prison where Joseph is confined. They appear one morning disturbed, puzzling over dreams which they can't understand. Joseph interprets the dreams, telling the wine steward that he will soon be released, and asking him, "Please remember me when everything is going well for you, and please be kind enough to mention me to the king and help me get out of this prison" (40:14, GNB). The baker, however, will soon be executed. All happens, just as Joseph had said. And what happens to Joseph? Our hopes are raised, when we hear that the wine steward is back in his position, but he forgets his promise, and for two more years Joseph is left in prison.

In telling this part of Joseph's story, these chapters have something to say about life in relationship to God. There can be times of success and blessing, when everything goes right (39:1–6). But even for God's people, there can be times of suffering, suffering which is not deserved (40:15). Such is the way life is, even life with God.

Then one night Pharaoh had a pair of strange dreams. Seven fat cows were grazing along the Nile. Then seven thin cows came and ate them up. Pharaoh woke up, then went back to sleep and dreamed again. There were seven full heads of grain, and then seven thin ones grew up and swallowed the full ones. When none of his wise men could explain these dreams, the wine steward remembered Joseph. The Hebrew slave is brought before Pharaoh, who says, "I have been told that you can interpret dreams." Joseph gives proper credit, saying, "I cannot, Your Majesty, but God will give a favorable interpretation" (41:16, GNB).

Joseph does interpret the dreams. Seven good years in Egypt will be followed by seven years of famine. The king must prepare for such by assigning someone to develop a grain storage program which will store up food for the future. And so it happens that Joseph is put in charge of the program. Pharaoh gives him a royal ring, puts a royal robe on him (the third robe in the story, now giving evidence of Joseph's position of power), gives him his own government vehicle, and appoints him governor over all of Egypt. Now the story tells how Joseph becomes totally Egyptian. He takes an Egyptian name and has an Egyptian wife. He is the highest official, under the Pharaoh, in the Egyptian government. For seven years, everything goes as Joseph had said. The crops are good, and the Egyptians store up grain. Two sons are born to Joseph and his wife. But then, the famine strikes and "People came to Egypt from all over the world to buy grain from Joseph, because the famine was severe everywhere" (41:57, GNB).

Before moving to the next section of the story, we pause to observe what the story is saying about God and human events. Once Joseph made the future known, Pharaoh and his administrative machinery went into immediate action. Gerhard von Rad comments on this:

> What is theologically noteworthy is the way in which the strong predestinarian content of the speech is combined with a strong summons to action. The fact that God has determined the matter, that God hastens to bring it to pass, is precisely the reason for responsible leaders to take measures![8]

The story is now taking place in the midst of the world of politics, government policies, and intense economic activity. The details of the complex grain storage program were worked out by Joseph, and administered through the instruments of Egyptian bureaucracy. All of this takes place in an ordinary, methodical way. But directing it is Joseph, the one of whom we have been told, "The LORD is with him." In such ways, according to this narrative, God works his purposes out; through gifted individuals, in this case an individual in a position of power and influence in the government. At a later point in the story, the narrator makes clear what was really happening when Joseph says, "It was really God who sent me ahead of you to save people's lives" (Gen. 45:5, GNB). Joseph was wise and gifted and developed a plan which saved the lives of many. But the giver of these gifts, the story makes clear, is God (41:16).

Joseph and His Brothers: Shalom Restored (Genesis 42–45)

The first part of the Joseph story took place in the land of Canaan. The setting for the second part has been Egypt. Now the two are brought together, as Joseph's brothers travel from Canaan to get food in Egypt.

Our story has said "the famine was severe everywhere" (41:57, GNB). That included Canaan. Now it is Jacob who makes a suggestion to his sons: "Why don't you do something? I hear that there is grain in Egypt; go there and buy some to keep us from starving to death" (42:1–2, GNB). Soon the brothers will meet, but this time the balance of power has changed. The once powerless young brother now represents the most powerful government of the day:

> Joseph, as governor of the land of Egypt, was selling grain to people from all over the world. So Joseph's brothers came and bowed down before him with their faces to the ground. (42:6, GNB)

With this detail, the teller of the story would have us remember Joseph's dreams. Then the action is slowed down. The encounter between Joseph and his brothers is put in the form of a dialogue. The text reads like the script for a play, with a narrator, Joseph, and the brothers:

Narrator:	When Joseph saw his brothers, he recognized them, but he acted as if he did not know them. He asked them,
Joseph:	(harshly)"Where do you come from?"
Brothers:	"We have come from Canaan to buy food."
Narrator:	Although Joseph recognized his brothers, they did not recognize him. He remembered the dreams he had dreamed about them.
Joseph:	"You are spies; you have come to find out where our country is weak."
Brothers:	"No, Sir! We have come as your slaves, to buy food. We are all brothers. We are not spies, sir, we are honest men."
Joseph:	"No! You have come to find out where our country is weak."
Brothers:	"We were twelve brothers in all, sir, sons of the same man in the land of Canaan. One brother is dead, and the youngest is now with our father."
Joseph:	"It is just as I said. You are spies. This is how you will be tested: I swear by the name of the king that you will never leave unless your youngest brother comes here. One of you must go and get him. The rest of you will be kept under guard until the truth of what you say can be tested. Otherwise, as sure as the king lives, you are spies." (42:7–16, adapted from GNB)

We might think about how this whole incident appeared from the standpoint of the ten brothers. Shepherds from a rural country, they have arrived in the capital city of the world's greatest empire. When they finally have a chance to meet the man in charge of grain distribution, they are falsely accused. Though innocent, they are put into prison for three days. Think of the questions they must have had: what have we done? what kind of country is this? what sort of people are these Egyptians? how long will we be held?

After three days they are released, and brought before Joseph. "One of you must stay here," he says, "but the others can go free." The brothers have been speaking to Joseph through his Hebrew interpreter. Since they assume the "Egyptian" cannot understand them they say:

"Yes, now we are suffering the consequences of what we did to our brother; we saw the great trouble he was in when he begged for help, but we would not listen. That is why we are in this trouble now." (42:21, GNB)

Something was happening to the brothers. They acknowledge their guilt, in connection with what they had done to their brother twenty years earlier! When they speak to one another in Hebrew, Joseph understands every word. He must excuse himself, goes out, breaks down and cries.

Simeon is left as hostage in Egypt, and the brothers start out toward home, but then some strange things begin to happen. Along the way, one of them opens his sack to get feed for his donkey and discovers that his money has been put back! They interpret this theologically, "What has God done to us?" (42:28, GNB). When they get home, they tell their father the whole story. Once again, they have to explain to him why one of them has not returned! In addition, they have to ask him to risk the life of Benjamin, Joseph's full brother, in order to get Simeon back. Then when they open their sacks, they discover that all of their money has been returned. It is almost too much for the old father:

> "Do you want to make me lose all my children? Joseph is gone; Simeon is gone; and now you want to take away Benjamin. I am the one who suffers!" (42:36, GNB)

Jacob had kept Benjamin at home in the first place because he was worried that something might happen to him, and now they want to take him away!

But the famine gets worse, and the family needs food. Jacob is in a no-win situation it seems, the classic doublebind. If he does nothing, they will starve. If he sends Benjamin to Egypt, Jacob is sure that he will never see his youngest son again. Finally he says, "If that is how it has to be, then take the boy and go!" Luther has a comment on Jacob's action here:

> This is an illustrious example, and we should follow it in all our actions and in our whole life. For when we have done all that was possible in our tribulation and distress—just as Jacob here opposed the plans and wishes of his sons with great zeal—and there has been no help in those means, then indeed we should say: "Well and good! I have done what I could. I have not tempted God. As for the rest, I must rely on the promise He has given and entrust everything to His will and good pleasure." Then you will have the most rightful excuse of necessity, and God will liberate you in a wonderful manner or will certainly give you something better than you could foresee. Only do not lose heart.[9]

Jacob sends his sons to Egypt with a present, and a prayer:

> "... take the best products of the land in your packs as a present for the governor: a little resin, a little honey, spices, pistachio nuts, and almonds. ... Take your brother and return at once. May Almighty God cause the man to have pity

on you, so that he will give Benjamin and your other brother back to you. As
for me, if I must lose my children, I must lose them." (43:11–14, GNB)

As soon as they arrive, they are summoned to Joseph's house. When the
brothers hear of this invitation, they are afraid, fearing that it has something to
do with the money in their sacks. The minute they get in the door, they
explain to the servant that the money has been returned, but he says:

> "Don't worry. Don't be afraid. Your God, the God of your father, must have
> put the money in your sacks for you. I received your payment." (43:23, GNB)

That announcement must have unnerved them all the more.

At noon, Joseph comes to eat with them. They bow down, and we who
hear the story are to recall the dreams once again. Joseph is courteous: "How
are you all? How is your old father?" Then he sees his brother Benjamin. It is
almost too much for him, and he excuses himself for a moment. But he regains
his composure and the meal is served.

As the brothers take their places, another uncanny thing happens. They
look at the place cards, and discover that they are seated in order of their age!
How could this man have known such details? What sort of investigative
system does this powerful government have? We could imagine one brother
whispering, "I'll be glad when we get out of here!" and another answering, "*if*
we get out of here!" And Benjamin, for some reason, is served five times as
much as anyone else.

The next day the brothers get up early, ready to make the trip home, but
Joseph is not through with them yet. He sets up a situation which will test
them. He tells his servant to return each man's money, placing it in the top of
his sack. Then he instructs him to put his silver cup in the sack belonging to
Benjamin. When the brothers are just a short way out of the city the servant,
on Joseph's orders, intercepts them:

> "Why have you paid back evil for good? Why did you steal my master's silver
> cup? It is the one he drinks from, the one he uses for divination. You have
> committed a serious crime!" (44:4–5, GNB)

The brothers deny the charge and say, "Sir, if any one of us is found to have it,
he will be put to death, and the rest of us will become your slaves" (44:9,
GNB). The servant answers,

> "I agree; but only the one who has taken the cup will become my slave, and the
> rest of you can go free." (44:10, GNB)

They lower their sacks to the ground. The search begins, starting with the sack belonging to the oldest brother. Then, one by one, each of the others. The brothers must have felt relieved, every time another sack passed the inspection. But then, in the very last sack, the one belonging to Benjamin, the cup was found!

Now we should pause to look at the situation through the eyes of Benjamin's brothers. They could have left Benjamin with the slave, and gone home. They could have explained very easily to their father what had happened: as far as they knew, young Benjamin, carried away by the splendor and excitement of a magnificent dinner in luxurious surroundings, took the cup! They could have said, "Dad, he must have taken it. He just couldn't resist. We couldn't help it! It wasn't our fault. It's his problem!" They could have gone home and left Benjamin in Egypt.

But they didn't.

Once before, when a brother was in trouble they had left him behind (42:21). Now they have changed. They turn around and head back to the city.

The brothers are brought to Joseph's house. Just the night before, they had been guests at a banquet. Now they are returning as suspected thieves. Again, they bow down before Joseph, and we remember the dreams. Joseph accuses them of theft, and then Judah speaks for all:

> "What can we say to you, sir? . . . How can we argue? How can we clear ourselves? God has uncovered our guilt. All of us are now your slaves and not just the one with whom the cup was found." (44:16, GNB)

Joseph says:

> "Oh no! I would never do that! Only the one who had the cup will be my slave. The rest of you may go back safe and sound to your father." (44:17, GNB)

Joseph is testing them once again. He has contrived a situation similar to the one in which they found themselves twenty years earlier. They could abandon a brother, return to their father, and this time give an explanation which leaves them in the clear. They could go home and leave Benjamin behind.

Again, they don't.

Now Judah steps forward, to speak to the great man of Egypt. Think of the scene: a shepherd, addressing the second most powerful man of his time! Judah's speech is a long and moving one. The point is made in the request at the conclusion:

> "And now, sir, I will stay here as your slave in place of the boy: let him go back
> with his brothers." (44:33, GNB)

For the sake of the well-being of the community, one member of the community offers to take the punishment which properly belongs to another. The biblical reader cannot but be reminded of the figure of the servant who takes upon himself the punishment which others deserve (Isa. 40–55) or, indeed, of a Galilean whose life fit that servant pattern (the Gospels).

No answer is given to Judah's eloquent request. Joseph sends everyone out of the room, leaving the brothers alone with him. Then he speaks to them:

> "I am Joseph. Is my father still alive?" But when his brothers heard this, they
> were so terrified that they could not answer. Then Joseph said to them, "Please
> come closer." They did, and he said, "I am your brother Joseph, whom you sold
> into Egypt. Now do not be upset or blame yourselves because you sold me here.
> It was really God who sent me ahead of you to save people's lives." (45:3–5,
> GNB)

Here the storyteller, who is reluctant to speak about God intervening in human events, speaks very clearly about God. The theological point of the whole story is made three times, in just a few verses, repeating the verb, "sent": "It was really God who sent me ahead of you. . . . God sent me ahead of you. . . . So it was not really you who sent me here, but God" (45:5, 7, 8). Gerhard von Rad writes:

> Here in the scene of recognition the narrator indicates clearly for the first time
> what is of paramount importance to him in the entire Joseph story: God's hand
> which in all the confusion of human guilt directs everything to a gracious goal.
> After so much has been said exclusively about men's actions, it is surprising for
> Joseph in two statements to mention God as the real subject of the whole
> occurrence; God, not the brothers, "sent" Joseph here . . . the question of how
> this activity of God is related to the brothers' drastically described activity re-
> mains an absolutely unsolved mystery. The matter must rest with the fact that
> ultimately it was not the brothers' hate but God who brought Joseph to Egypt
> and moreover "to preserve life."[10]

The tension of the family story thus finds its resolution. The shattering of shalom, the breakup of peace, the jealousy, the envy, are all drowned out, in the sounds of the weeping and the laughter of the reunited brothers. We have said that the family story has been shaped into a guidance story. That theme is stated clearly: "So it was not really you who sent me here, but God" (45:8, GNB). The same guidance theme is sounded again at the end of the Joseph material. Jacob has died and the brothers ask, "Will Joseph now turn against us?" They go to him, asking forgiveness, once again bowing before him. But Joseph says:

> "Don't be afraid; I can't put myself in the place of God. You plotted evil against me, but God turned it into good, in order to preserve the lives of many people who are alive today because of what happened." (Gen. 50:19–20, GNB)

With this, the story has come to its conclusion.

For a New Time

Whatever else we may say about it, the story of Joseph is a good story. This has been recognized by those who continue to retell it in new forms, from Thomas Mann's multi-volumed *Joseph and His Brothers* to Marc Chagall's series of paintings and Webber and Rice's musical, *Joseph and the Amazing Technicolor Dreamcoat*.

As part of Scripture, we expect to hear in the Joseph story some word of direction for faith and life. How could we summarize what this story has to say to our own time?

1. Considering it as a family story, we are struck by its humanity. We have already noted that the picture of family life as given here is not idealized. The years of the life of this family are "laden with happiness and tears." When we encounter jealousy, deception, conflict in our own families, we should not find this surprising. Such is the stuff out of which human life is made. Such is the way families are. The Joseph story can remind us of that and can keep us from despairing when our own families don't seem to measure up to the smiling, embracing groups that we see on the jackets of books devoted to "the Christian family."

A friend once remarked to me, "There are corners of heaven and pits of hell that people without children don't even know about." At the end of the Joseph story, the aged Jacob meets Pharaoh in the Egyptian court. Pharaoh asks, "How many are the days of the years of your life?" The old man answers, "The days of the years of my sojourning are a hundred and thirty years; few and evil have been the days of the years of my life . . ." (Gen. 47:8–9). This answer, says Westermann, "is the ripe fruit of his experience with God. He has learned that the one who is blessed remains a human being, with the limits and failings which human beings have. . . . He had been blessed with many sons, but the blessing had brought bitter pain."[11] Jacob knew the "pits of hell" that are part of parenting, as well as some of the corners of heaven.

2. Reflecting on the Joseph story as a guidance story, we discover that it has something to say about God and human events.

First, consider the fact that there is a remarkable absence of religious language in the story. We hear nothing of prayer, of worship, or religious activities. Neither the storyteller nor the characters speak often of God. Yet, at the opportune moment, a theological point will be made (41:16; 45:7–9; 50:20). There have always been some among the people of God who can say confidently, "The Lord led me here" or "The Lord told me to do this," but there are others who are more reluctant to speak of God's involvement in the everyday. The teller of the Joseph story is one of these. As Westermann has said, "We do not need to be more pious in our exposition than the Joseph story itself is" in describing what it says about God.[12] And what does it say? That God works through ordinary people, through their meeting and greeting, caring and acting. In such a way the Joseph story understands God's relation to human events, and we can understand that relationship in the same way.

We have called attention to the passages in chapters 45 and 50 which sound the theological theme explicitly: God was working his purpose out, through the lives of Joseph and his family. As we seek to discern the working out of his purposes in our own lives, we ought at the outset to free ourselves of a misunderstanding. Once again, this story is refreshing in its realism. God is "not the dear God of pious history where everything always goes right."[13] Joseph did the faithful and right thing in refusing Potiphar's wife, but that landed him in jail for two long years! The life of the believer carries no guarantee that everything will always go right.

But there is a guarantee, and that is that God will always go *with* us. We have noted the emphasis on this theme in Genesis 39. The "with-ness" of God is another way of speaking about his blessing (Gen. 39:21). That preposition "with" is a powerful one. I can recall walking through a dark underground tunnel alongside a small son. When it became pitch dark, a hand stretched out to take that of his father. The darkness was still dark, but it made a great deal of difference to that boy to know that in that darkness someone was *with* him. The same preposition occurs in the middle of the twenty-third psalm. Again, we see that the life of the believer is not one where "everything always goes right." The psalmist says, "Even though I walk through the valley of the shadow of death, I fear no evil; for thou art with me . . ." (Ps. 23:4). We can follow this preposition, which binds God and people like a father's hand taking that of a child, through the Bible. According to the last chapter of Matthew, Jesus' final word to his disciples was a promise, "and lo, I am *with* you always, to the close of the age" (Matt. 28:20, author's italics). The first chapter of that same Gospel tells us that it was Jesus himself who bound God and people together: " 'and his name shall be called Emmanuel' (which means, God with us)" (Matt. 1:23). We continue to hear that promise in our worship, "The Lord be with you," and in the hymn "God be with you, 'til we meet again." Our word for parting, "Goodbye," is a shortened form of, "God be with you."

How does God relate to human events? On the worldwide scale, this story tells us how he works through gifted leadership, "to save people's lives." On the individual scale, we find the biblical theme of the "with-ness" of God.

3. Long ago I heard an aged pastor preach a sermon about God's guidance. He recalled that as a boy, he once sat on the floor, looking up at the bottom side of an embroidery hoop upon which his mother was sewing. Viewed from underneath, the whole thing appeared to be a mess, with knots, breaks, twists, turns, threads going this way and that, but when his mother picked him up and he viewed the hoop from the top, he saw how all the threads were woven into a beautiful pattern. And so, said this pastor, it is with God and our lives: he can pick up the breaks, the knots, the twists, and weave them into a pattern with meaning and even beauty.

"PURPOSE Irregular" was the indication for the tune and meter of the hymn which provides the title for this chapter. "How true" was the comment by some theologically inclined editor at *The New Yorker*. How true, indeed! The Joseph story is filled with irregularities, as are other stories in the Bible— and the stories of our lives, too. All of these stories also witness to the fact that God works with and through such irregularities, whether to save many lives from famine, or, as in the Gospel story, to seek and to save those who are lost.

CHAPTER 5

Tales from the Wild, Wild West Bank

Judges 6—8; 13—16

Those who have grown up in the United States have often heard the story of "how the west was won." The settlement of this country was a movement from the east into the west, with the frontier gradually expanding. This period of the youth of our nation generated its heroes, and legends grew up around them. Names such as Daniel Boone and Davey Crockett, Kit Carson and Calamity Jane, Wild Bill Hickock, Wyatt Earp, and Buffalo Bill Cody bring to mind many a tale, and perhaps even a ballad or two. The popularity of stories from the days of the "wild, wild west" is evidenced by the continuing existence of "western" novels on paperback bookstands and by the western movies which continue to play in theaters and on television.

The settlement of Israel was also a movement from the east, across the Jordan River, into the west. That settlement began about 1240 B.C. For about two hundred years, the people lived in the land without a king. These were the frontier days for Israel, and these times produced a series of heroes whose exploits were the subject of story and song. These leaders of Israel were called "judges." Among them were figures like Othniel and Ehud, Shamgar and Deborah, Gideon, Jephthah, and Samson. Travelers told stories about them as they rested by watering places (Judg. 5:10–11). The Bible preserves a ballad about one of them (Judg. 5). Claus Westermann's comments about the period of the judges could be a description of the frontier days of our own nation. Speaking of the book of Judges, he writes:

> . . . it describes a nation's youth, a wild, effervescent and often exuberant period, when they lived for the moment, a period in which inspiration counted more than sober planning, the daring deed born of the moment more than a clever system of government. It was a time in which joking, wild spirits and audacity had their place. . . .
>
> This, too, then is not lacking in our Bible; the youth of a nation with its merry-making, its unconcern and its inspiration belong to the history of the people of God and has its place in it.[1]

The New Testament records a sermon in which the great heroes of the faith are listed, one after another. We hear of Abel, Enoch, Noah, Abraham and Sarah, Isaac, Jacob, Joseph, Moses, and Rahab. Then the preacher ran out of time, and he had the good sense to cut his sermon short. But he does tell us that if time had allowed, he would have preached about Gideon, Barak, Samson and Jephthah (Heb. 11). What would he have said if he had told about Gideon and Samson? We shall have to listen to those stories, and then try to make our own guess.

The Deuteronomistic History

Before getting to the stories themselves, it is necessary that we place them in their broad literary context. They are a part of that long, connected historical work which modern scholarship calls the "Deuteronomistic History" (DH).[2]

1. This historical work, you will recall, consists of the books from Deuteronomy through 2 Kings, with the exception of Ruth. The book of Deuteronomy begins with the people poised on the east bank of the Jordan, ready to enter the promised land, but first they hear a series of addresses by Moses:

> In this book are the words that Moses spoke to the people of Israel when they were in the wilderness east of the Jordan River. (Deut. 1:1, GNB)

This historical work ends with a description of how King Jehoiachin is released from captivity in Babylon, in "the thirty-seventh year after Jehoiachin had been taken away as prisoner" (2 Kings 25:27, GNB). The date when Jehoiachin was taken to Babylon was 597 B.C. Thus the DH covers the period from about 1240 B.C. (forty years after the Exodus) to 560 B.C., or some 780 years. With the ending of 2 Kings, the DH comes to a conclusion. The next book, 1 Chronicles, begins a new telling of the biblical story: "Adam was the father of Seth."

2. How can a knowledge of this DH help us to understand the stories which we find in the book of Judges? If, in its present form, this is a connected work from the hand of one author, then we have a date for the final composition of the DH. Since the last event mentioned took place in 560 B.C., the work must have been composed sometime after that date. Most likely the time for the production of the final edition of the DH was during the exile (587–539 B.C.), when the people of Judah were in Babylon. The DH was then addressed to the exilic situation.

We might surmise that the writer had at his disposal a number of ancient materials, many of which had existed at first in oral form but now were written down. These materials from the youth of the nation included some tales from a period which we call the time of the judges and some carefully composed accounts from the time of the monarchy. The author-editor put these together, adding editorial comments of his own. Like a modern scholar, he tells us at a number of points, "If you want to know more about this, you can read about it in _____" (for example 1 Kings 14:19, 29, etc.).

What was the exilic situation which the author as addressing? We remember that in 587 B.C. Jerusalem was burned, the temple was destroyed, and the majority of the citizens of Judah were taken to live as prisoners of war in Babylon. The political history of the once-proud nation, the glory of the days of David and Solomon, had all come to and end. Biblical materials coming from this exilic period provide us with some clues as to the mood of the people. Psalm 137 says:

> By the rivers of Babylon we sat down;
>   there we wept when we remembered Zion. . . .
> Those who captured us told us to sing;
>   they told us to entertain them:
>   "Sing us a song about Zion."
> How can we sing a song to the LORD
>   in a foreign land? (Ps. 137:1–4, GNB)

The psalmist is asking, "How can we worship when our church has been destroyed? Can we sing praises to God without sacrifices or temple?"

We can also get something of the mood of the people in Babylon by listening to the prophet of the exile, whose words we find in Isaiah 40–55. He picks up words that he has heard as he has moved among his people, quoting those words in his sermons:

> Why do you say, O Jacob,
>   and speak, O Israel,
> "My way is hid from the LORD,
>   and my right is disregarded by my God"? (Isa. 40:27)

And, on another occasion:

> But the people of Jerusalem said,
>   "The LORD had abandoned us!
>   He has forgotten us." (Isa. 49:14, GNB)

Those people in exile were discouraged, wondering whether they could still sing hymns of praise to their God in this strange and far-off land. They were disenchanted, asking why a gracious God had let his temple be destroyed and his people be deported. The questions remain familiar ones: "Pastor, why did God let this happen to us? Pastor, what shall we do next?"

The prophet-pastor whose words we find in Isaiah 40–55 addressed these questions, but so did the author of the DH. Here is a message addressed to a people perplexed about their present and puzzled about their future.

3. One theme runs through this long composition. It is sounded clearly at the end of the book of Deuteronomy. Moses says to the people:

> "Today I am giving you a choice between good and evil, between life and death. If you obey the commands of the LORD your God . . . then you will prosper and become a nation of many people. . . . But if you disobey and refuse to listen, and are led away to worship other gods, you will be destroyed—I warn you here and now. You will not live long in that land across the Jordan that you are about to occupy." (Deut. 30:15–18, GNB)

The historical writer then goes on to tell the story of Israel in the promised land. Time after time the people disobey and start to worship other gods. Time after time they suffer the consequences of such apostasy. An especially clear example of his technique in historical writing may be found in 2 Kings 17. The historian describes the fall of Samaria, the capital of the northern kingdom, to the Assyrians (2 Kings 17:1–6). But then he adds his own comments:

> Samaria fell because the Israelites sinned against the LORD their God. . . .
> They worshiped other gods. (2 Kings 17:7, GNB)

In this way the author, who is really a theologian and a preacher, deals with that question of the exiles: "Why did this happen?" His answer is: "God has not forsaken you. It was you who have forsaken him, time and again! And you've known since the time of Moses that if you chose to worship other gods, you would be taken off the land!"

4. How does the author of the DH use the material which he has placed in the book of Judges? We assume that these stories about frontier heroes from various tribes of Israel first circulated in oral form. He has picked them up, reshaped them, and readdressed them to the situation of his hearers in exile. If you look carefully at the book of Judges, you can see how he has worked. He is dealing with stories about six major judges. He places each of these stories into a framework, which is his own composition. For a clear example of this framework, note the account about the first of the judges, Othniel:

(1) The people forget the Lord and worship idols (Judg. 3:7)

(2) The Lord allows enemies to conquer them (3:8)

(3) The people cry to the Lord for help (3:9)

(4) The Lord sends a deliverer to free them (3:9–11).

Note how this framework may be detected in the accounts of each of the judges:

	Othniel	Ehud	Deborah	Gideon	Jephthah	Samson
(1)	3:7	3:12	4:1	6:1	10:6	13:1
(2)	3:8	3:12–14	4:2	6:1–6	10:7–9	13:1
(3)	3:9	3:15	4:3	6:6–7	10:10–16	–
(4)	3:9–11	3:15–30	4:4–5:31	6:11–8:32	10:17–12:7	13:2–16:31

Element 4 is expanded in the case of each of the judges, depending upon what material the author had at his disposal or how he wanted to use it. The Jephthah story gives us an insight into the nature of element 3. This consists of both a statement of repentance, "We have sinned against you, for we left you, our God, and worshiped the Baals" (10:10, GNB) and a cry for help, " . . . please, save us today" (10:15, GNB).

Now imagine yourself hearing these stories in exile. You are puzzled: "Why are we here? Has God forsaken us and forgotten about us? In these stories you have example after example of your own people's history of apostasy, followed by an account of how the Lord gave them over to enemies. What would that mean for you? First, you would see that it was not God who had forsaken his people, but his people who had forsaken him. What should you do next? In terms of the author's framework, you and your people are now at element 2. Now, if you repent and cry for help (element 3), perhaps God in his amazing grace will once again send a deliverer! In such a way this historian-preacher uses these old stories to speak to a new time.

Gideon

We have already alluded to the famous sermon in Hebrews 11, where the preacher says, "Should I go on? There isn't enough time for me to speak of Gideon, Barak, Samson, Jephthah ... " (vs. 32, GNB). The preacher had Gideon in the outline for his sermon, in the company of Abraham and Sarah, Isaac, Jacob, and the rest. What might he have said about him?

1. The stories about Gideon have been gathered in the book of Judges, chapters 6–8. The Deuteronomistic historian has taken up some very ancient tales about this young Israelite farmer and has fit them into the framework that we have identified in the previous section of this chapter. The Gideon story begins with the simple statement which is element 1 of the framework:

> Once again the people of Israel sinned against the LORD .... (Judg. 6:1, GNB)

Then comes the second element of that framework:

> ... so he let the people of Midian rule them for seven years. (Judg. 6:1, GNB)

The Midianites were distant relatives of the Israelites, tracing their ancestry back to Abraham through his third wife, Keturah (Gen. 25:2). They settled in the area to the east of the Gulf of Aqaba. By the time that the Israelites were settled in their land, the Midianites had successfully domesticated the camel, which gave them a great advantage in raiding and waging war. John Bright writes about their use of the camel, as mentioned in the Gideon stories:

> This is the earliest instance of such a phenomenon of which we have record. The effective domestication of the camel had been accomplished somewhat earlier deep in Arabia and had now spread to tribal confederacies to the south and east of Palestine, giving them a mobility such as they had never had before. Israelites, terrorized by these fearsome beasts, fled in panic. Since the raids apparently came annually at harvest time, the situation soon became desperate; had not something been done, Israel might well have been permanently crippled.[3]

The narrator tells us that these Midianites with their camels were joined by Israel's long-time enemies the Amalekites (Exod. 17:8–9; see also Judg. 10:12) and by other desert tribes. The Israelites had to hide in caves to save their lives. The situation was dire, indeed! The storyteller expands upon element 2 of the Deuteronomistic framework:

> The Midianites were stronger than Israel, and the people of Israel hid from them in caves and other safe places in the hills. Whenever the Israelites would plant their crops, the Midianites would come with the Amalekites and the desert tribes and attack them. They would camp on the land and destroy the crops as far south as the area around Gaza. They would take all the sheep, cattle, and donkeys, and leave nothing for the Israelites to live on. They would come with their cattle and tents, as thick as locusts. They and their camels were too many to count. They came and devastated the land, and Israel was helpless against them. (Judg. 6:2–6, GNB)

The narrative continues with element 3 of the framework for these stories: "Then the people of Israel cried out to the LORD for help against the Midianites" (Judg. 6:7, GNB). The first response of the Lord to this cry was the sending of a prophet. To understand the prophet's word, we should remember that these stories, as part of the DH, are being addressed to a people in exile. One of their questions was, "Why are we here? Has God forsaken us?" The prophet's statement speaks to that question. He said:

> "Thus says the LORD, the God of Israel: I led you up from Egypt, and brought you out of the house of bondage; and I delivered you from the hand of the Egyptians, and from the hand of all who oppressed you, and drove them out before you, and gave you their land; and I said to you, 'I am the LORD your God; you shall not pay reverence to the gods of the Amorites, in whose land you dwell.' But you have not given heed to my voice." (Judg. 6:8–10)

The first part of this prophetic message was a reminder of what God had done for his people when he delivered them from Egypt and gave them their land, but the real point is in the second part: these people had not been loyal to the Lord but had worshiped the gods of the land where they had settled. To the person in exile, this prophetic word said: "Why are you in exile? Not because God has forsaken you, but because you have forsaken God!"

But this was not the only way in which the Lord responded to the cry of his people. After the negative word brought by the prophet comes element 4 in the pattern of these stories, the account of the sending of a deliverer.

2. The narrator says "Then the LORD's angel came to the village of Ophrah and sat under the oak tree that belonged to Joash . . . " (Judg. 6:11, GNB). This is a different world from that of the Joseph story! There were no

angels there; God worked his purposes out through ordinary people and everyday events. An angel was mentioned in the story about matchmaking in Genesis 24, but no one ever saw the angel. However, here the angel or messenger
(this is what the word means) comes and sits under an oak tree. He must have
looked like an ordinary person, because Gideon saw nothing unusual about
him. Now imagine the scene and listen in on the conversation between this
messenger and Gideon, putting yourself in the place of a young Israelite—
maybe in your late teens or early twenties—in exile in Babylon.

Gideon is threshing wheat. Ordinarily the job would be done in the open,
so that the wind could blow the chaff away and the grain would fall to the
ground, but because of the Midianite problem, this young farmer has to do his
threshing in secrecy, working down in a pit used for crushing grapes to make
wine. A stranger walks over to the edge of the pit, looks down at Gideon, and
says, with a certain irony:

> "The LORD is with you, you mighty man of valor." (Judg. 6:12)

This pious talk is too much for Gideon. He looks up and replies:

> "Pray, sir, if the LORD is with us, why then has all this befallen us? And where
> are all his wonderful deeds which our fathers recounted to us saying, 'Did not
> the LORD bring us up from Egypt?' But now the LORD has cast us off, and
> given us into the hand of Midian." (Judg. 6:13)

This conversation furnishes the key to understanding the way in which the
Deuteronomistic historian is using this old story from the time of the Judges
to address the new situation of the exile. As Gideon looks up from his work
down there in the hole dug for pressing grapes, his question becomes the
question of those in exile: "If the Lord is with us, then what are we doing here
in exile?" His is a question about the Lord, a theological question. That question, in fact, becomes the question of any honest believer, brought up in the
faith, respecting the religion of family and forebears, but unable to deal with
the realities of a present situation: if the Lord really is with us, why has this
happened? To put his question into a modern idiom Gideon asks, "If the Lord
is with us, what am I doing in the pits?"

Gideon's theological questions are not answered. The "why" and the
"where" are left hanging. But Gideon is given a task, as this stranger begins to
speak to him in the first person: "Go in this might of yours and deliver Israel
from the hand of Midian; do not I send you?" (Judg. 6:14). Gideon responds
with a "Who, me?" and begins to list reasons why he could not be the deliv-

erer. His family is not well-known! And besides, he is the youngest one in that family! Then, after indicating the task, the messenger makes a promise: "But I will be with you . . . " (Judg. 6:16).

Long after the time of Gideon, another young man was once addressed by the Lord. When the word of the Lord came to Jeremiah saying, "I appointed you a prophet to the nations," he could only reply, "Ah, LORD GOD! Behold, I do not know how to speak, for I am only a youth" (Jer. 1:6). And to that objection also came only the announcement of a task, coupled with a promise:

> "Do not say, 'I am only a youth';
> for to all to whom I send you you shall go,
> and whatever I command you you shall speak.
> Be not afraid of them,
> for I am with you to deliver you,
> says the LORD." (Jer. 1:7–8)

The questions remain questions. The objections are overruled. For Gideon, then for Jeremiah, what remains is the task, and the promise, "I will be with you."

2. Gideon's task was to deliver his people from the Midianites. He began by trimming down the size of his army:

> The LORD said to Gideon, "The men you have are too many for me to give them victory over the Midianites. They might think that they had won by themselves, and so give me no credit. Announce to the people, 'Anyone who is afraid should go back home, and we will stay here at Mount Gilead.' " So twenty-two thousand went back, but ten thousand stayed. (Judg. 7:2–3, GNB)

The army was still too large, and so Gideon took the men down to a stream, telling them to get a drink. Most of them put their faces down into the water, but a few scooped the water in their hands and drank it. These were the best soldiers, alert even while pausing for water, and they became Gideon's crack tactical group of three hundred.

The biblical story gives evidence of the careful military planning that went into the operation. Israelite intelligence had discovered that rumors of defeat were abroad in the Midianite camp (Judg. 7:13–14). Gideon's plan itself was a daring and somewhat outlandish utilization of psychological warfare. He divided his three hundred men into three groups, giving each man a trumpet and a jar with a torch inside it. He told the men:

> "When I get to the edge of the camp, watch me, and do what I do. When my

group and I blow our trumpets, then you blow yours all around the camp and
shout, 'For the LORD and for Gideon!' " (Judg. 7:17–18, GNB)

The attack was to take place at night, just after the changing of the Midianite
guard (7:19). Gideon's army had the advantages of darkness, fighting in their
own territory, and surprising the enemy just at the time when the guard had
been changed. One can imagine a good deal of drilling with the jars, trumpets,
and torches, and careful practice so that the whole operation would be executed
with perfect timing! The biblical account reports:

> Gideon and his one hundred men came to the edge of the camp a while
> before midnight, just after the guard had been changed. Then they blew the
> trumpets and broke the jars they were holding, and the other two groups did
> the same. They all held the torches in their left hands, the trumpets in their
> right, and shouted, "A sword for the LORD and for Gideon!" Every man stood
> in his place around the camp, and the whole enemy army ran away yelling.
> While Gideon's men were blowing their trumpets, the LORD made the enemy
> troops attack each other with their swords. (Judg. 7:19–22, GNB)

After this initial attack, Gideon summoned help from the rest of the tribes of
Israel. Finally, after many a bloody battle, the Midianites were defeated. The
Deuteronomistic historian wraps it up with the familiar summary: "So Midian
was defeated by the Israelites and was no longer a threat. The land was at peace
for forty years, until Gideon died" (Judg. 8:28, GNB).

3. What implications could this old story have for our time? We can begin
by simply listening to the tale about Gideon. It is a good one, with plenty of
excitement. The young, skeptical farmer becomes the leader of an army of
three hundred which defeats thousands! We can hear the story as a child might
hear it, enjoy it, and learn that God delivers his people from their enemies.

The way in which the story has been incorporated into the Deuteronomistic history gives us a clue as to how it addressed those in exile. We have seen
that the editor has placed it into his framework, with the elements of apostasy,
the attack of enemies, the people crying to the Lord, and deliverance brought
about by a "judge." If you were a Jew living in exile, this retelling of the story
would carry meaning for you. Why has all this happened to us? Because we
have forsaken the Lord. The collection of stories in Judges makes this point
clear. What should we do next? These stories indicate that when God's people
have been in trouble, they have always cried to the Lord for help. And time
and again he has helped them! Perhaps if we do the same, in his amazing
grace, he will deliver us once again!

There is, however, a deeper level at which this story can address our time. The clue is found in that question about God, that theological question which Gideon asks:

> "Pray, sir, if the LORD is with us, why then has all this befallen us? And where are all his wonderful deeds which our fathers recounted to us . . . ?" (Judg. 6:13)

Listen carefully to that question. Notice that it is raised by one who has been brought up in the faith. He has heard the "wonderful deeds" of the Lord from his elders. But now it seems that the God of his fathers and mothers has forsaken him. The Lord may have done some great things way back then, but he surely doesn't seem to be doing much right now!

Such, we have seen, was the mood of those in exile. We still hear their voices saying, "My way is hid from the LORD" (Isa. 40:27) or "The LORD has forsaken me, my Lord has forgotten me" (Isa. 49:14). We can still hear them singing, "How shall we sing the LORD's song in a foreign land?" (Ps. 137:4).

Other voices of the Bible pick up Gideon's question. The psalms of lament throw their "why's" and "how long's" toward heaven:

> How much longer will you forget me, LORD? Forever? . . . How long must I endure trouble? (Ps. 13:1–2, GNB)

> My God, my God, why have you abandoned me? (Ps. 22:1, GNB)

The most radical of the questioners is the writer of Ecclesiastes. He finally concludes that we just can't know what God is doing:

> As you do not know how the spirit comes to the bones in the womb of a woman with child, so you do not know the work of God who makes everything. (Eccl. 11:5)

Gideon's theological questions are not answered. The Lord's response is the assigning of a task, "Go . . ." and the making of a promise, "I will be with you." We find this same task-promise pattern at other places in the Bible.

After the resurrection, Jesus' eleven disciples were with him in Galilee. They had questions and doubts: "When they saw him, they worshiped him, even though some of them doubted" (Matt. 28:17, GNB). But the Gospel reports no discussions, no answering of the theological questions. Jesus simply assigns them a task:

> "Go, then, to all peoples everywhere and make them my disciples: baptize them

in the name of the Father, the Son, and the Holy Spirit, and teach them to obey everything I have commanded you." (Matt. 28:19–20, GNB)

And then he leaves them with a promise:

"And I will be with you always, to the end of the age." (Matt. 28:20, GNB)

The apostle Paul, trying to carry out his task, was ejected from the synagogue in Corinth. His work there, it seemed, was finished. But, in a vision, the Lord recalled him to his task:

"Do not be afraid, but keep on speaking and and do not give up." (Acts 18:9, GNB)

And then he left him with a promise:

". . . for I am with you." (Acts 18:10, GNB)

The apostle was encouraged and sustained by that promise of the "with-ness" of God, and he picked it up and relayed it to congregations all over the Mediterranean world, so that they might be encouraged and sustained, too:

The God of peace be *with* you all. (Rom. 15:33, author's italics)

The grace of the Lord Jesus Christ and the love of God and the fellowship of the Holy Spirit be *with* you all. (2 Cor. 13:14, author's italics)

Gideon's questions received no answers. The doubts of the disciples were not resolved. The opposition to Paul continued. The questions remained questions, the doubts remained doubts. The Lord's response was a task, and a promise, "I will be with you." This was enough to sustain Gideon, the disciples, and the evangelist. Transposed into a new key by the One whose name was "God with us" (Matt. 1:23), that promise can sustain and encourage us in our tasks, too.

Samson

Biblical interpreters often seem to be at a loss when faced with the Samson materials. In his Table Talk, Luther remarked, "I often wonder about the example of Samson. There must have been a strong forgiveness of sins in his case."[4] A recent popular introduction to the Old Testament simply bypasses the Samson stories, saying:

It is unnecessary to go into the details of these lusty stories, which have as their theme the discomfiture of the Philistines by an Israelite Tarzan whose fatal weakness was women.[5]

Another theologian reports some of the allegorizing interpretations of Samson, but then concludes: "Such allegorizing is, of course, out of the question for us; and beyond this kind of literary-allegorical pursuit of the Samson saga we are able to find nothing."[6]

Despite the perplexity which Samson provokes among scholars, he remains a popular figure. What child doesn't remember the Samson stories and the colored pictures of his exploits in a Bible story book or a Sunday school handout! Artists have been fascinated by Samson. Rembrandt has given us "Samson's Wedding Feast," "Samson Threatening His Father-in-Law," and "The Blinding of Samson." One of Albrecht Dürer's woodcuts is of "Samson and the Lion." In his book *Lord Grizzly*, novelist Frederick Manfred introduces a tale of mountain men with a quotation from the Samson story, drawing a parallel between this biblical figure and the rugged individualists from the days of the western frontier in the United States.[7] Finally, we recall that something about Samson would have been included in that sermon in Hebrews 11, except for the fact that the preacher was running out of time (Heb. 11:32)! Thus, despite the problems he has caused for scholarly interpreters, the love for the Samson stories in popular piety and the fact that he is mentioned as a fitting theme for a Christian sermon encourages us to listen to this tale from the wild, wild west bank.

1. The Samson story begins with the typical elements of the framework furnished by the editor-composer: "The Israelites sinned against the LORD again" (element 1), "and he let the Philistines rule them for forty years" (element 2: Judg. 13:1, GNB). In order to understand these tales, we must have some knowledge of these aggressive and warlike neighbors of Israel.

The Bible itself tells where the Philistines originally came from: "The LORD says . . . 'I bought the Philistines from Crete and the Syrians from Kir . . .'" (Amos 9:7, GNB). They were among the "peoples of the sea," coming from the island of Crete, and settling on the southeast coast of the Mediterranean, shortly before the arrival of the Israelites. They lived principally in five cities: Gaza, Ashkelon, Ashdod, Ekron, and Gath. A glance at a map indicates that the Israelite tribe of Dan, to which Samson's family belonged, was settled along their northern border and Judah along the eastern border. The area where they lived was called "Philistia." Eventually that name was applied to the whole of the territory west of the Jordan in the form "Palestine."

What were these Philistines like? The most famous of them is remembered in the biblical story of Goliath. He is described as follows:

A man named Goliath, from the city of Gath, came out from the Philistine camp to challenge the Israelites. He was over nine feet tall and wore bronze armor that weighed about 125 pounds and a bronze helmet. (1 Sam. 17:4–5, GNB)

He had a spear, we are told, with an iron head which weighed fifteen pounds and was attended by a soldier who walked ahead of him, carrying his shield. This is the way the biblical tradition remembers the Philistines! John Bright describes them as:

> . . . a military aristocracy which ruled a predominately Canaanite population . . . [the Philistines were] formidable fighters with a strong military tradition. . . . They were, moreover, disciplined soldiers whose weapons, owing especially to their monopoly on iron, were superior.[8]

The gigantic Goliath was an accurate symbol of Philistine power and might!

We know from the biblical records that the Philistines eventually defeated the Israelites and that because of them, Israel was driven to a monarchical form of government. The stories about Samson take place in the years before full-scale war broke out (1 Sam. 4), on the border between the settlements of the Israelites and the Philistines.

2. This time the element in the framework, "the people cried to the LORD" is not present. The Lord simply initiates the act of deliverance himself. He sends a messenger to a young woman to tell her, "Behold, you are barren and have no children; but you shall conceive and bear a son "(Judg. 13:3). This is to be a special child, dedicated to the Lord, "and he shall begin to deliver Israel from the hand of the Philistines" (Judg. 13:5).

This language sounds very much like another birth story in the Bible. Once again, a messenger from God appears to a young woman and tells her, "And behold, you will conceive in your womb and bear a son . . . " (Luke 1:31). This child will be called Joshua, or Jesus, which means "one who saves," "for he will save his people from their sins" (Matt. 1:21). In both instances, God initiates his acts of deliverance by announcing the birth of a child.

The boy was to be brought up as a Nazirite. Among the requirements for those who were part of this religous group is the following:

> As long as he is under the Nazirite vow, he must not cut his hair or shave. . . . His hair is the sign of his dedication to God. (Num. 6:5–6, GNB)

According to the narrative, the young woman and her husband were not sure that this person had been sent from God. But when they offered a burnt offering, they saw him go up to heaven in flames. Then they knew: this was God's messenger. The child was born, "and the boy grew, and the LORD blessed him. And the Spirit of the LORD began to stir him ..." (Judg. 13:24–25). Again, the story is reminiscent of what was said about Jesus (Luke 2:40, 52).

3. The first of the tales about Samson tells how he got his wife. One day he went to the little town of Timnah and met a Philistine girl. He went home and told his parents, "There is a Philistine girl down at Timnah who caught my attention. Get her for me; I want to marry her" (Judg. 14:2, GNB). The parents, understandably, feared this kind of mixed marriage. This gifted son of theirs, whose birth had been announced by a messenger from God, wanted to marry outside his own traditon and faith! Weren't there plenty of fine young Israelite women around for him to choose from? With such a mother, how could they hope that any children would be brought up in the faith? So they said, "Why do you have to go to those heathen Philistines to get a wife? Can't you find a girl in our own clan, among all our people?" (Judg. 14:3, GNB). But Samson had his mind made up and his parents, probably realizing that they couldn't stop it anyway, went along with his wishes and made arrangements for the wedding.

At this point the biblical storyteller lets us in on something that the parents were not aware of:

> His parents did not know that it was the LORD who was leading Samson to do this, for the LORD was looking for a chance to fight the Philistines. At this time the Philistines were ruling Israel. (Judg. 14:4, GNB)

Here is a word to parents despairing over the seemingly foolish actions of a son or daughter: it could be that God has some plans for this child that you don't know about!

The story continues by telling of a riddle and a bet. On the way to Timnah, Samson had heard a lion roar. "The Spirit of the LORD came mightily upon him" (Judg. 14:6), the text says, and he killed the lion with his bare hands. A few days later as he walked down the road he saw the carcass of the lion. Some bees had made a hive in it, and he scraped out some honey and ate it.

All of this gave Samson the inspiration for a riddle, and a wager. When he got to Timnah he found a group of Philistine men. He said, "Here's a riddle. I'll bet you can't guess it before the week of the wedding feast is over. If you do, you each get a new suit of clothes" (Judg. 14:12–13, author's paraphrase). They took him on, and he gave them this riddle:

> "Out of the eater came
>   something to eat;
> Out of the strong came
>   something sweet." (Judg. 14:14, GNB)

These Philistines were friends of Samson's bride. When they couldn't figure out the answer, they tried to get it out of her, and she began to work on her husband. She said, "You don't love me! You just hate me! You told my friends a riddle and didn't tell me what it means!" (Judg. 14:16, GNB).

Samson wouldn't tell her. She kept nagging him and, we are told, cried for the whole week of the wedding feast. Clearly Samson's marriage was off to a shaky start! Finally, the young husband could take no more and told his wife the answer. She, of course, told her friends, and they told Samson. He knew how they had discovered the answer and said,

> "If you hadn't been plowing with my cow,
> You wouldn't know the answer now." (Judg. 14:18, GNB)

Then, once again, "the Spirit of the LORD came mightily upon him" (Judg. 14:19), and Samson went down to the Philistine town of Ashkelon. There he killed thirty men, took their suits, and paid off his bet. And so, the story tells us, Samson began to deliver his people from the Philistines.

4. There are other tales told about Samson.

They still remember him in Ashkelon. A number of years ago I visited that modern resort city on the Mediterranean Sea and was reminded of Samson. On the wall of the dining room of the Hotel Ashkelon was a huge mural, in grays, blues, and flaming reds. It pictured foxes with flaming torches tied between their tails. The story behind the incident is told in Judges 15. Because Samson had been neglecting his new Philistine wife, her father gave her to someone else. When Samson came to see her, his father-in-law said, "I really thought that you hated her, so I gave her to your friend. But her younger sister is prettier, anyway. You can have her, instead" (Judg. 15:2, GNB). This suggested solution to his marital problems was not satisfactory to Samson, and he decided to get back at the Philistines. He caught three hundred foxes. Then he tied torches in their tails and sent them into the fields and orchards of the Philistines. The story says, "In this way he burned up not only the wheat that had been harvested but also that wheat that was still in the fields" (Judg. 15:5,

GNB). Then, says the story, he killed a few more Philistines and retreated from action for a time.

One time the Philistines made a raid on the town of Lehi. Again, "the Spirit of the LORD came mightily upon him" (Judg. 15:14) and Samson picked up the jawbone of a donkey. Using it as a weapon, he killed another thousand Philistines (Judg. 15:9–20).

Then there was the time that Samson went to the Philistine city of Gaza. He walked into town, met a prostitute on the street, and went to bed with her. The Bible continues the tale:

> The people of Gaza found out that Samson was there, so they surrounded the place and waited for him all night long at the city gate. They were quiet all night, thinking to themselves, "We'll wait until daybreak, and then we'll kill him." (Judg. 16:2, GNB)

Samson surprised them. He stayed with the prostitute only until midnight. He burst out of her house and then, in an amazing feat of strength, ripped the city gate loose from its mooring. He hoisted the massive structure onto his shoulders and in a prank that was never to be forgotten, hauled it all the way to Hebron, some forty miles distant (Judg. 16:1–3)!

The most well known of the stories about Samson is that about his unfortunate affair with Delilah. This time a Philistine woman would be the undoing of him. He fell in love with her, and when the Philistines found out about it, they convinced her to act as a double agent.

Three times Delilah asked Samson the secret of his strength. Each time he told her the wrong answer. But she kept at it:

> "How can you say you love me, when you don't mean it? You've made a fool of me three times, and you still haven't told me what makes you so strong." (Judg. 16:15, GNB)

She kept after him, day after day, until he told her, "I have been dedicated to God as a Nazirite from the time I was born. If my hair were cut, I would lose my strength and be as weak as anybody else" (Judg. 16:17, GNB).

Now Delilah knew her lover's secret. Some time later, the two were together and she lulled the unsuspecting Samson to sleep. She held his head gently on her lap. Then she called in an accomplice who cut off his hair. Samson's strength was gone. The Philistines captured him, blinded him, and put him to work grinding in the prison. As time went on, the story tells us, his hair started to grow back.

Once at a great festival celebrating the god Dagon, the Philistines were making fun of their blinded captive. Kings from all five Philistine cities were present, as well as some three thousand people. Samson prayed to the Lord, pushed on the pillars which supported the building, and the whole structure collapsed. The five kings were killed as well as all the others. Samson was killed, too, and the story ends with the account of his burial.

5. What are we to make of these tales about this "Israelite Tarzan" as we ask about their meaning for our time? At first level, we ought to recognize that here are collected some stories about a hero from the frontier days of a young nation. As is the case with other such stories, we ought to expect a good deal of embellishment and embroidering as they were told and retold, but let us not tone down the person of Samson! With his long flowing hair, he must have been a memorable figure, striding fearlessly into this Philistine stronghold or that, making his bets, playing his pranks, getting involved in love affairs with a variety of Philistine women. We see Samson in these stories in much the same way that we see some of the figures from the frontier days of our own nation.

These wild and woolly tales have been taken up and incorporated into our Scripture. We have detected the comments of the editor in the typical framework and in the remark about the Lord's involvement in Samson's mixed marriage (Judg. 14:4). These old stories were being used to address a new time, that of the exile.

What would they have meant to the Jews held captive in Babylon? Obviously, the situations of the Israelites in the time of Samson and in the time of the exile were similar. They were the underdogs, in each case nearly helpless in the face of a superior power. Then it was the Philistines, now it was the Babylonians. That group of captives must have cheered when they heard these tales! Samson was one of their own! They must have laughed when they heard of his pranks and applauded when the jawbone of an ass was a weapon mightier than any the Philistines had, even with their monopoly on iron! They understood what these stories meant: as God was able to deliver our people once before, so he is able to deliver us!

But do these old Samson stories have a word for our time? Can we imagine what that sermon in Hebrews 11 might have said about him?

First of all, we shall have to take Samson as he is. We cannot allegorize him or try to find secret meanings in his actions. We cannot use him as an example, because so much of what he did was not exemplary! Samson must remain Samson, proposing riddles, playing pranks, making love. These stories can then remind us of the fact that the Bible shows us people as they are, not as they ought to be, and God could use this Samson, with his minuses as well as his plusses! He is never depicted as a puppet, with God pulling the strings. Samson remains Samson, passionate, impetuous, with a great love for life. God used him as he was.

These stories would call us to trust in God, despite outward appearances. No doubt Samson's parents spent many a sleepless night, worrying about their son and wondering about his next escapade. No doubt these pious believers were heartbroken when he married outside the faith. But, the narrator tells us, "it was the LORD who was leading Samson to do this . . . " (Judg. 14:4). Samson was their son, but he was God's, too.

These stories would remind us to make room for the spontaneous and unplanned, the bold deed and the daring act. "The Spirit blows where it wills," the New Testament tells us (John 3:8, RSV margin) and in the case of Samson, the Spirit blew him into a series of most remarkable adventures (Judg. 13:25; 14:6, 19; 15:14)!

Finally, these stories suggest that we ought not to be too quick to judge or dismiss the unusual or eccentric person from the company of God's people. No doubt most of us would be quite uncomfortable with a Samson on the membership rolls of our congregation. He was a prankster, a gambling man, and had an inclination toward the bawdy. His antics are remembered in Ashkelon, to this day; he is also remembered in the roll call of the heroes of the faith, in the company of such as Abraham and Sarah, Moses, and David! If God could use a person like Samson then, who knows what sort of person God might be using now? We, like those of Samson's time, might be surprised.

CHAPTER 6

Two Love Stories

Ruth

The story told in the book of Ruth is a farmer's story. It begins by telling of crop failure and a family which had to leave their home place and try to make a living in a new land. One of the scenes takes place during the barley harvest. We see the men and women working in the fields, stopping for a break in the heat of the day, and the widows and poor people picking up the scraps which are left behind. Another scene takes place out where the men are threshing. If you are a farmer, or have worked or lived on a farm, you will have an inside track on understanding this story.

This story is also a family story. The major focus is not on the nation Israel, nor on God and God's relationship to the other nations of the world. The focus here is on one family; more accurately, on a part of a family. The main characters as the story begins are three women. The first loses a husband, then two sons. The others are her widowed daughters-in-law. If you are a woman, particularly a woman who has lost a loved one, you will have special insight into what is told here.

Finally, this is also a love story. It tells about a bachelor farmer, getting on in years, and a beautiful young stranger who comes to his town. But more is told in these pages. Woven in with the story of Ruth and Boaz is another love story. We shall listen for it, as the tale unfolds.

Some Preliminaries

The setting for the story itself is clearly indicated in the opening words: "In the days when the judges ruled . . ." (1:1). Here is another tale from the time when the nation was young, from Israel's frontier days as she was settling the "wild, wild west bank." After hearing of the military exploits of Gideon and the bawdy escapades of Samson, we now encounter this idyllic story of life in the little town of Bethlehem. This is a story taken from everyday life in a rural village, where the men and women work together in the fields and where nothing extraordinary seems to happen. There are no great battles or ringing speeches. These are ordinary people, coping with problems like crop failure or the loss of a spouse or a son and celebrating events like the birth of a child.

When was the story of Ruth written down? Scholarly opinion has swung back and forth on this issue. Many have believed that it must have been written down sometime after the exile (587–539 B.C.). Its intention was to counter the harsh attitude of Ezra and Nehemiah toward marriage with foreigners (see Ezra 10:1–5; Neh. 13:23–27). More recently, some have argued that a story which tells of the Moabite ancestry of David must be earlier than Deuteronomy 23:3–6 (usually dated in the seventh century B.C.) which speaks in a harshly negative way about Moabites. During a time as late as the post-exilic period, it is argued, such an ancestry would have been passed over in silence. (Compare the suppression of the Bathsheba incident in 1 Chron. 20; vs. 1 starts by following 2 Sam. 11:1, but then skips around the Bathsheba affair to 2 Sam. 12:26.) Along with this argument, recent scholarship has noted the absence of direct divine intervention in the story, whether through angels, visions, or words from God, and has suggested that it was composed during the early monarchy, perhaps reflecting the secular spirit of the time of Solomon (961–922 B.C.).

Since David is mentioned in the last sentence, the story must have been put into its final form sometime after he became king. Because of the recording of David's Moabite ancestry and because of the restraint with which the story speaks of the involvement of God in everyday affairs, resulting in a theological tone similar to that of the Joseph story, it seems reasonable to think of the final edition of the story as appearing in the time of King Solomon (961–922

B.C.). Once again an old story, which grew out of events during the time of the judges, is reshaped to address a new time.

The book is structured around four scenes, one in each chapter. The first takes place on the road to Bethlehem (1:6–18), the second in the field of Boaz (2:1–17), the third at the threshing place (3:6–15), and the last at the city gate (4:1–12). The introduction tells of crop failure and of death and loneliness in the family, setting forth the tension: how will these widows survive (1:1–5)? The conclusion announces a birth and resolves the tension with the picture of a joyful mother and grandmother, surrounded by caring friends. The story is linked to the larger biblical story by identifying the child as the ancestor of David (4:13–22). In between the major scenes are short transitions reporting the actions and conversations of Ruth and Naomi (1:19–22; 2:18–23; 3:1–5; 3:16–18).

On the Road Again

The story begins with the statement, "there was a famine in the land." The rains did not come. There was no crop. First one year, and then the next. And so a young farmer and his wife made a difficult decision: they would leave their home place and seek a new life in a new land. Taking their two sons with them, Elimelech and his wife, Naomi, packed up their belongings, said good-bye to family and friends, and set out down the road which led out of Bethlehem to the neighboring country of Moab.

The biblical storyteller uses the device of time acceleration when giving an account of what happened in Moab. Apparently things must have gone well for a while because the family lived there for ten years. Then more tragedy. Elimelech died, leaving Naomi a widow with two sons to raise. These two sons met Moabite women and married them. But Naomi was to experience more grief. First one of her sons died, and then the other. The three women were left, alone: Naomi, and her daughters-in-law, Orpah and Ruth.

Such is the situation as the book of Ruth begins. The tension which will drive the story is introduced: how will these three women survive, without husbands? It is difficult for a widow to make her way alone today, and it was particularly difficult then.

The story gets going with the announcement that "Some time later Naomi heard that the LORD had blessed his people by giving them good crops . . ." (1:6, GNB). We might observe that in only two places in the whole story of Ruth does the narrator speak about God.[1] In neither case do we hear about any dramatic delivering or rescuing operation, such as we found in the stories in

Judges. Rather, the narrator speaks of God's action of blessing. The word "bless" does not occur in the Hebrew text, but the idea is present, and the GNB translation catches the sense very well: "Naomi heard that the LORD had blessed his people by giving them good crops . . ." (1:6). The other place which speaks of the Lord is at the end of the story. Once again, the GNB translation aptly supplies the word "bless," even though it is not found in the Hebrew: "The LORD blessed her, and she became pregnant and had a son" (4:13). As was the case in the Joseph story, the storyteller is sparing in the use of God-talk. When he does speak of the Lord, it is important to notice what is being said. In these two passages, which frame the story, we hear about the quiet, unnoticed, action of God's blessing: he causes the crops to grow, and he enables Ruth and Boaz to have a child.

When Naomi got word that things were better in Bethlehem she made another decision. She packed her belongings and said goodbye to her friends in Moab. Her two daughters-in-law started out with her. She was on the road again, this time heading back toward Bethlehem.

On the road from Moab to Bethlehem we have the setting for the most well-known words from the story of Ruth. Naomi tells the two young women with her, "Go back home and stay with your mothers. May the LORD be as good to you as you have been to me and to those who have died. And may the LORD make it possible for each of you to marry again and have a home" (1:8, GNB). Remember Naomi's prayer that these two might marry again! We shall discover that it is answered, in the course of the story.

Ruth and Orpah kissed Naomi goodbye, and they all began to weep. The two daughters-in-law didn't want to leave Naomi, and they said, "We will go with you to your people." When Naomi urged them to go back home, Orpah did so. But Ruth said:

> "Don't ask me to leave you! Let me go with you. Wherever you go, I will go; wherever you live, I will live. Your people will be my people, and your God will be my God. Wherever you die, I will die, and that is where I will be buried." (1:16–17, GNB)

We should pause to notice that this was a most courageous statement of loyalty and friendship on Ruth's part. She was still young, in her twenties, and was now ready to break ties with her own family, her homeland, and her religion, to take up a new life in a strange country with her mother-in-law. Phyllis Trible comments on the radical nature of this decision:

From a cultural perspective, Ruth has chosen death over life. She has dis-
avowed the solidarity of family; she has abandoned national identity; and she
has renounced religious affiliation. In the entire epic of Israel, only Abraham
matches this radicality, but then he had a call from God.[2]

Naomi is on the road again. Ten years earlier she had traveled this road
with a husband and two young sons, on her way to a new life in a new land.
Now she walks the road as a widow, with a widowed daughter-in-law by her
side.

When the two of them arrive in Bethlehem, word gets around fast and
soon the whole town is buzzing. The women there ask, "Is this really Naomi?"
She answers,

> "Don't call me Naomi [which means 'pleasant'] . . . call me Marah [which
> means 'bitter'], because Almighty God has made my life bitter. When I left
> here, I had plenty, but the LORD has brought me back without a thing. Why
> call me Naomi when the LORD Almighty has condemned me and sent me
> trouble?" (1:20–21, GNB)

The first part of the story now comes to a close, with a statement in which
the storyteller summarizes what has happened thus far, and points ahead to
what will follow:

> This, then, was how Naomi came back from Moab with Ruth, her Moabite
> daughter-in-law. When they arrived in Bethlehem, the barley harvest was just
> beginning. (1:22, GNB)

The story as told to this point has been a sad one, telling of crop failure,
famine, death in the family, and three women, trying to make it in the world
alone. It is no wonder that Naomi would say, "Call me Marah!" But now, for
the first time, a positive note is struck: the harvest is just beginning!

In the Field of Boaz

In order to understand the next scene in the story, we should know something about the way in which ancient Israel cared for the widow, the orphan,
and the poor. Legislation providing for their welfare is preserved in the books
of Deuteronomy and Leviticus:

> "When you gather your crops and fail to bring in some of the grain that
> you have cut, do not go back for it; it is to be left for the foreigners, orphans,
> and widows, so that the LORD your God will bless you in everything you do.
> When you have picked your olives once, do not go back and get those that are
> left; they are for the foreigners, orphans and widows. . . . Never forget that you

were slaves in Egypt; that is why I have given you this command." (Deut. 24:19–22, GNB)

When you harvest your fields, do not cut the grain at the edges of the fields, and do not go back to cut the heads of grain that were left; leave them for poor people and foreigners. The LORD is your God. (Lev. 23:22, GNB)

A similar practice, I have been told, has continued to exist among the potato farmers of the Red River Valley in Minnesota. The potato picking machines cannot dig in the extreme corners of the fields. Occasionally, potatoes are dropped and left lying on the ground. The poor are then allowed to dig in the corners and pick up those potatoes which have been left.

The scene is introduced with a conversation between Ruth and her mother-in-law:

One day Ruth said to Naomi, "Let me go to the fields to gather the grain that the harvest workers leave. I am sure to find someone who will let me work with him."

Naomi answered, "Go ahead, daughter."

So Ruth went out to the fields and walked behind the workers, picking up the heads of grain which they left. It so happened that she was in a field that belonged to Boaz. (2:2–3, GNB)

We should pause to notice what is said in the last sentence above. The RSV translates, "and she happened to come to the part of the field belonging to Boaz." A very literal translation of the Hebrew would read, "and her chance chanced upon" or "her luck lucked upon." The same vocabulary occurs in the story telling how the ark of the Lord was captured and taken into Philistine territory. While it was there, the Philistines began to get tumors and die. They put the ark on a cart, pulled by a team of cows, and let the cows take it wherever they would. The Philistines said:

if it goes toward the town of Beth Shemesh, this means that it is the god of the Israelites who has sent this disaster on us. But if it doesn't, then we will know that he did not send the plague; it was only a matter of *chance*. (1 Sam. 6:9, GNB, author's italics)

The same language is also used in the story about the young man who happened to come upon the dying Saul on Mount Gilboa. He told David, "*By chance I happened* to be on Mount Gilboa . . ." (2 Sam. 1:6, author's italics). Use of this vocabulary clearly indicates that the storyteller was saying, "By chance, she happened to come to the part of the field belonging to Boaz." But is that what is really meant? As the story develops, we discover that the narrator means just the opposite. Naomi has prayed that Ruth might find a husband (1:9). Here, in the ordinary course of day-by-day events, a "chance" meeting takes place which turns out to be the answer to that prayer. In such ways prayers are answered, the story means to show. Ruth heard no voice telling her to go here or there. She saw no vision of the field of Boaz. She just "happened" to go there. But in that happening, God was active in answering the prayer of a caring mother-in-law.

And now Boaz enters the story. Who was he? "A rich and influential man" (2:1, GNB), says the story, who was a relative of Naomi's husband, Elimelech. Later on we learn that he was no longer young, but getting on in years (3:10). This wealthy bachelor farmer comes out to see how things are going in one of his fields. On the way he notices a stranger, a young woman, working with the other widows and poor people. He asks his foreman:

> "Who is that young woman?"
> The man answered, "She is the foreign girl who came back from Moab with Naomi. She asked me to let her follow the workers and gather grain. She has been working since early morning and has just now stopped to rest for a while under the shelter." (2:5–7, GNB)

This young woman is a hard worker! Boaz walks over to speak with her, telling her:

> "Let me give you some advice. Don't gather grain anywhere except in this field. Work with the women here; watch them to see where they are reaping and stay with them. I have ordered my men not to molest you. And whenever you are thirsty, go and drink from the water jars that they have filled." (2:8–9, GNB)

Ruth responds:

> "You are very kind to me, sir. You have made me feel better by speaking gently to me, even though I am not the equal of one of your servants." (2:13, GNB)

Then, after Ruth and the others had gone out to continue working, Boaz called some of his own men aside:

> "Let her gather grain even where the bundles are lying, and don't say anything to stop her. Besides that, pull out some heads of grain from the bundles and leave them for her to pick up." (2:15–16, GNB)

The new woman in the field had clearly caught the attention of this bachelor farmer! Perhaps it was her beauty, perhaps her industry, her humility, or maybe her "fascinating Moabite accent."[3] In any case, Boaz saw to it that she was taken care of, and told his men to drop some extra grain in the area where she was working, so that she could pick it up.

When Ruth went home that night, she had nearly twenty-five pounds to show for her day's work. And when Naomi asked her where she had been, Ruth told her, "in a field belonging to a man named Boaz" (2:19, GNB). When she hears this, Naomi the complainer changes her tone.

"The LORD always keeps his promises to the living and the dead" (2:20, GNB), she says, and she advises Ruth to keep working in the field of Boaz. She does, until the harvest is over. And then a plot begins to form in that mother-in-law's matchmaking head. She had prayed that Ruth might marry again. Now it was time for her to couple that prayer with action.

At the Threshing Place

One day Naomi said to her daughter-in-law, "I must find a husband for you, so that you will have a home of your own" (3:1, GNB). As we hear Naomi saying this, we ought to remember that some time earlier she had said, "And may the LORD make it possible for each of you to marry again and to have a home" (1:9, GNB). It would appear that with this statement in 3:1, the narrator wants us to recall that prayer of Naomi. At this point the story provides an instructive commentary on the relationship between prayer and action. Naomi had prayed that the Lord would give Ruth a husband and a home. "The LORD" was the subject of the sentence. He would "make it possible." Now the subject is "I"; "I must find a husband for you." When faced with a family problem, Naomi prays. But she also goes into action, with a plot which showed imagination, and which involved a good deal of risk! Naomi said to Ruth:

> "Remember that this man Boaz, whose women you have been working with, is our relative. Now listen. This evening he will be threshing the barley. So wash yourself, put on some perfume, and get dressed in your best clothes. Then go where he is threshing, but don't let him know you are there until he has finished eating and drinking. Be sure to notice where he lies down, and after he falls asleep, go and lift the covers and lie down at his feet. He will tell you what to do." (3:2–4, GNB)

Ruth does just what her mother-in-law tells her. The action occurs at the threshing place, a cleared, flat area outside the village where the wind would blow freely, so that the chaff would be driven away and the grain would fall to the ground. The story continues:

When Boaz had finished eating and drinking, he was in a good mood. He went
to the pile of barley and lay down to sleep. Ruth slipped over quietly, lifted the
covers and lay down at his feet. During the night he woke up suddenly, turned
over, and was surprised to find a woman lying at his feet. "Who are you?" he
asked.
      "It's Ruth, sir," she answered. "Because you are a close relative, you are
responsible for taking care of me. So please marry me." (3:7–9, GNB)

Boaz, barely awake and no doubt quite surprised to find that a woman has
crawled under the covers with him, speaks to her, in the darkness and quiet of
that night out at the threshing place:

      "The LORD bless you. . . . You might have gone looking for a young man,
      either rich or poor, but you haven't." (3:10, GNB)

    The older bachelor is flattered that the fascinating young stranger has not
gone chasing after one of the "young bucks running around in tight-fitting
jeans."[4] It would appear that the story's tension is close to being resolved, and
that Ruth will find a husband. But this bachelor farmer, who wants to do
things just right, brings up a technical point:

      "Now don't worry, Ruth. I will do everything you ask; as everyone in town
      knows, you are a fine woman. It is true that I am a close relative and am
      responsible for you, but there is a man who is a closer relative than I am. Stay
      here the rest of the night, and in the morning we will find out whether or not
      he will take responsibility for you. If so, well and good; if not, then I swear by
      the living God that I will take the responsibility. Now lie down and stay here
      till morning." (3:11–13, GNB)

Ruth has reminded him that, as a close relative, he had an obligation to care
for her. But Boaz points out that there is another relative who is even closer.
He has first choice in the matter. The directive regarding a family's care for a
widow is set forth in Deuteronomy 25:

      "If two brothers live on the same property and one of them dies, leaving no
      son, then his widow is not to be married to someone outside the family; it is
      the duty of the dead man's brother to marry her." (Deut. 25:5, GNB)

And so a complication arises. Ruth's marriage will not be arranged so simply.
We shall have to wait to see what happens. The matter will be handled properly, in due time, by the town court.
    Ruth spent the rest of the night with Boaz. But then, while it was still
dark, he awakened her and told her to be on her way before anyone could see

her. Their being together could be misunderstood by gossip-minded townspeople!

When Ruth got home, her mother-in-law was, as might be expected, full of questions. She had no doubt lain awake much of the night. She had probably done some more praying! She asked, "How did you get along, daughter?" and Ruth told her all that happened. The young woman, who had thought she might come back with a promise of marriage and the prospect of a new life in this land, was frustrated and disappointed. Boaz had to check first, with another relative! But Naomi calmed her down saying:

> "Now be patient, Ruth, until you see how this all turns out. Boaz will not rest today until he settles the matter." (3:18, GNB)

Now a new tension has been introduced into the story. What will happen at the court? What will the closer relative say?

At the Court in the Gate

In order to understand the final scene in the story, we should know something about cities in biblical times, and particularly about the function of the city gate.

The Bible indicates that there were both "walled cities" and "unwalled villages" (Lev. 25:29–31). Bethlehem was a walled city, and therefore had a city gate. Citizens of the town, most of whom made their living as farmers, lived inside the walls and worked the fields in the area surrounding.

Archaeologists have excavated some of these city gates. At Tell en-Nasbeh, for example, at the point where the gate was built the city walls met and then overlapped for some forty feet. The distance between the overlapping ends of the wall was forty feet. This would leave a square of forty by forty between the overlapping walls.[5] At the city of Dan, the square between the overlapping ends of the city wall was about sixty-seven by thirty-one feet.[6]

This area between the ends of the wall, which would be shut off by the closing of the gate, was the center for the city's activity. It is easy to imagine that this would be a place of buying and selling, meeting and greeting, saying hellos and goodbyes. In the morning workers going out to the fields would pass through the gate. In the evening they would come home the same way. We can imagine children waiting there for parents to return and old people sitting and watching what was going on.

One of the most important functions of the gate was the handling of legal matters. When Abraham purchased a burial place for his wife, the matter was settled "in the presence of the Hittites, before all who went in at the gate of his city" (Gen. 23:18). When family problems could no longer be handled by the family, the matter was brought before the "elders of the city in the gate" (Deut. 22:15; 21:19). Thus the gate was the equivalent to the court. Here was the place where justice was dispensed. The prophet Amos would say one day, "Hate evil, and love good, and establish justice in the gate" (Amos 5:15, which GNB rightly translates, "Hate what is evil, love what is right, and see that justice prevails in the courts").

This scene in the book of Ruth gives us a glimpse of what must have been an everyday occurrence in these cities. A legal matter had to be settled in court:

> Boaz went to the meeting place at the town gate and sat down there. Then Elimelech's nearest relative, the man whom Boaz had mentioned, came by, and Boaz called to him, "Come over here, my friend, and sit down." So he went over and sat down. Then Boaz got ten of the leaders of the town and asked them to sit down there too. (4:1–2, GNB)

At the excavations of the city gates of Dan and Gezer, the benches where the elders sat can be seen still.[7]

The matter was presented before the assembled court:

> "Now that Naomi has come back from Moab, she wants to sell the field that belonged to our relative Elimelech, and I think you ought to know about it. Now then, if you want it, buy it in the presence of these men sitting here. But if you don't want it, say so, because the right to buy it belongs first to you and then to me."
>
> The man said, "I will buy it."
>
> Boaz said, "Very well, if you buy the field from Naomi, then you are also buying Ruth, the Moabite widow, so that the field will stay in the dead man's family."
>
> The man answered, "In that case I will give up my right to buy the field, because it would mean that my own children would not inherit it. You buy it; I would rather not." (4:3–6, GNB)

The matter was settled. The nearest relative had been given his chance and turned it down. Boaz would take Ruth as his wife. Those gathered in the gate were witnesses to the procedure. And with this, the tension in the story, "How will Ruth find a husband?" is resolved.

The storyteller concludes things quickly, with a statement which accelerates time and wraps it all up. After describing the events of one day in court in some detail, nearly a year's time is compressed into one biblical verse: "So Boaz took Ruth home as his wife. The LORD blessed her, and she became pregnant and had a son" (Ruth 4:13, GNB).

The story began with Naomi sad and lonely. It ends with her surrounded by friends who care. They say:

> "Praise the LORD! He has given you a grandson today to take care of you. May the boy become famous in Israel!" (4:14, GNB)

The story began with Naomi returning to Bethlehem empty, having experienced too much death. It ends with her holding a baby in her arms. That baby, says a final note, would grow up to be the father of Jesse, and the grandfather of Israel's greatest king, David.

For a New Time

The story of Ruth has long been appreciated for its literary beauty. One can note the "emptiness" theme at the beginning, observe the gradual introduction of "fulness" with the coming of the harvest, and finally identify the complete reversal from emptiness to fulness with the birth of the child as the story ends. Because the story contains so much dialogue, it lends itself to dramatization on stage or screen. Here is a model short story, commendable for its craftsmanship, admirable in its artistry, and deservedly a favorite in "Bible as Literature" courses in high schools or colleges.

The Christian or Jewish reader has always come to this story expecting something more. It can be analyzed and appreciated. But, since it is part of Scripture, it can also be appropriated as an authoritative word from God, with something to say about God and people and also about relationships between human beings.

Many have understood the major impact of the story to be in this latter category. In sharp contrast to the negative attitude toward the foreigner expressed in Ezra and Nehemiah, this story puts a foreign woman in a most favorable light. The most memorable speech in the story is one which a Moabite woman gives: "Don't ask me to leave you! Let me go with you. Wherever you go, I will go . . ." (1:16–17, GNB). Her caring attitude is reminiscent of a story which Jesus told, about a foreigner from Samaria who helped out a man he found lying by the side of a road (Luke 10:25–37). Ruth stands as an example of loyalty and care and remains a worthy namesake for many a Jewish and Christian child!

The teller of this story also shows us how the little town of Bethlehem accepted this young Moabite widow as a full member of the community, and how in fact this foreigner became the great-grandmother of Israel's greatest king. The story of Ruth has a word to say about the attitude of the people of God toward the "outsider," and warns against any kind of self-centered superiority complexes, or tendencies toward exclusivism.

This story also has something to say about God and people, something which may be suggested by the title, "Two Love Stories." We have followed the love story about the lonely young widow meeting a wealthy, middle-aged bachelor farmer. Woven into that love story is another, about a God who heard the prayers of a widow who had had more than her share of grief. Here is a second love story, about a God who loves and who worked through the lives of the ordinary people in that small rural community to answer prayers and to bring about the marriage of Ruth and Boaz. It is at the theological level, where the story says something about God and people, where we find the most profound word for our own time.

Consider, for example, what we discover about prayer. The story gave us a hint of Naomi's prayer for her daughter-in-law, "May the LORD make it possible for each of you to marry again . . ." (1:9, GNB). This was a prayer sent forth from the midst of the activity of the everyday, on the dusty road leading back toward Bethlehem. No doubt Naomi prayed about the matter on other occasions, and in the story the prayer finds its answer, though we almost don't notice it. There are no voices from heaven, saying, "Ruth, go to the field of Boaz!" Ruth just "happens" to go to that field, but when we remember that prayer, we can see that in the working out of events in the lives of these people, God was pushing here, pulling there, quietly guiding these lives until the prayer did indeed find an answer. Therefore we can pray, the story suggests, on the roads of our lives, and we can look for answers to prayer, in the ordinary working out of things among the community of caring people.

Yet a final word must be said about this story, as we consider it in the broader context of the Bible as a whole. It is never retold in the New Testament, but in the first chapter of the first book of the New Testament, the name of this Moabite woman appears. Along with Tamar, Rahab, and the wife of Uriah (Bathsheba), Ruth is mentioned in the genealogy of Jesus. These four are an interesting company: Tamar, a non-Israelite who tricked her father-in-law by posing as a prostitute (Gen. 38); Rahab, another non-Israelite, a prostitute who sheltered some Israelite spies (Josh. 2); Bathsheba, the wife of a

Hittite soldier who became involved in a tawdry affair with David; and Ruth the Moabite. The mention of these four reminds us that God has worked through the lives of people as they actually are and that he is able to pick up the loose ends and torn threads of broken lives and weave them into a purposeful and meaningful design. The listing of Tamar, Rahab, Ruth and the wife of Uriah on the first page of the New Testament recalls for us that the message which follows is good news for all people, for those whose lives have taken some unusual twists and turns, for those "outsiders" who have no proud family connections with the company of the faithful. The first Gospel, which mentions these non-Israelites as it begins, also ends with a focus on the "outsiders": "Go therefore and make disciples of all nations . . ." (Matt. 28:19). The good news is for the lonely, the brokenhearted, the hurting, from all nations on the face of the earth. In such a way the New Testament picks up this second love story, hidden in the pages of the one about Ruth and Boaz, retells it for a new time, and fashions it into a story which concludes "(to be continued)."

CHAPTER 7

The Final Solution

Esther

The book of Esther is among the least familiar parts of the Old Testament, for Christian readers. In fact, it is difficult to find appreciative or positive comments for it. One standard introduction to the Old Testament says this of the book:

> But Christianity . . . has neither occasion nor justification for holding on to it. For Christianity Luther's remark should be determinative, a remark made with reference to II Maccabees and Esther in his Table Talk: "I am so hostile to this book and to Esther that I could wish they did not exist at all, for they Judaize too greatly and have much pagan impropriety."[1]

None of the church fathers wrote commentaries on Esther, nor did the Reformation commentators, Luther or Calvin. No readings from Esther appear in the Lutheran lectionary, either for Sunday worship or for day-by-day devotional reading, even though the latter contains selections from the Apocrypha.

For Jewish readers of the Hebrew Bible, Esther is among the most popular of the books. In the "Sabbath Prayer" from *Fiddler on the Roof,* Tevye can wish for his daughters, "May you be like Ruth and like Esther," pairing Esther with the great-grandmother of King David. I recall a conversation with a Jewish woman who proudly showed me a beautifully written scroll of Esther which she had kept in a rusting metal tube. She told me how it had belonged to her grandfather in Russia, and how Jews had come to his farm from miles around to hear the story of Esther read, each year at the time of the celebration of Purim.

The connection of the story of Esther with the festival of Purim accounts for the book's popularity among Jews. The story is retold each year in synagogues throughout the world. Rather, it is reenacted, with the listeners hissing Haman, the villain, and whirling noisy rattlers called "groggers" each time his name comes up in the story. At Purim time special cookies are made, called Hamantaschen, which recall the directive that these days are to be observed with "feasts and parties, giving gifts of food to one another and to the poor" (Esther 9:22, GNB).

Neglected by Christians, beloved by Jews, Esther has one characteristic which makes it different from any other book in the Bible. It makes no mention of God. Commenting on this, Elie Wiesel once said:

> Remember the Book of Esther which we read twice a year on Purim? God's name is not mentioned in that book. Not once. And the Talmud is wondering why? The answer, I believe, is at the end of the book where we are told that Jews, for a day or two, became avengers. God, I believe, says, "If this is so, my place is not there."[2]

What should be our approach to this old story? First of all, we point out the simple fact that it is part of Scripture. Despite his remark at table, Luther did translate the book and include it in his German Bible. If the book is such a favorite of Jews, could it be that Christians could learn something by noting how this community of faith uses it? We shall suggest that this is the case, and shall also suggest that it is precisely in the matter of relationships between Christians and Jews that this old story has something to say to our time.

Some Preliminaries

The opening sentence in the book of Esther indicates the setting for the action of the story:

> From his royal throne in Persia's capital city of Susa, King Xerxes ruled 127 provinces, all the way from India to Sudan. (1:1–2, GNB)

The reader of the Bible will perhaps remember that Persia dominated the ancient world after the period of the Babylonian Exile (587–539 B.C.). This story takes place in the city of Susa, east of the Tigris River, where the emperor had his winter residence. Xerxes is a person known from historical records, who ruled Persia from 486–465 B.C.

When was the story written down? Once again, the text itself provides us with no answer to this question. We are in an unusual situation with the book of Esther, in that we have a longer, Greek version of it (found in Protestant Bibles as the "Additions to Esther" in the Apocrypha) as well as the Hebrew one. We might reconstruct the composition of these two versions of Esther somewhat as follows:

1. The earliest stage was that in which stories about Esther circulated orally. If we assume that there was some historical core to the story, as seems reasonable, these stories would have arisen immediately after the events themselves.

2. A second stage resulted in the text as we have it in the Hebrew Bible and in the Protestant Old Testament. The oral material was shaped into a story, with certain embellishments, some things added, and others left out, to suit the purpose of the storyteller. We note that the action of the story comes to an end with chapter 9, verse 16:

> The Jews in the provinces also organized and defended themselves. They rid themselves of their enemies by killing seventy-five thousand people who hated them. But they did no looting. (GNB)

After this statement, we have directions for the celebration of Purim, in 9:17–19 and 9:21 to the end of the book. This indicates that by the time the story was taken into the Bible, it was already connected with the Purim celebration.

3. An expanded version of Esther was composed for Greek-speaking Jews near the end of the second century B.C. The Greek version concludes with a note referring to the translator as one "Lysimachus, son of Ptolemy, a member of a Jerusalem family" (Postscript to Greek Esther, GNB). Since this seems to refer to Jews who were living at the end of the second century B.C., we are able to date the Greek translation.

These additions are interesting because they show us how the story was retold and reinterpreted for a new time. Their major effect is to theologize the story. In the Hebrew version, God was not mentioned, nor were there any references to piety or prayer, but in the Greek retelling, much is said about God. In the introduction, Mordecai tells of his dream:

Then two huge dragons appeared, ready to fight each other. They made a dreadful noise, and all the nations got ready to make war against God's nation of righteous people. . . . All of God's righteous people were troubled, in great fear of what was about to happen to them. They prepared for death, but they cried out to God for help. In the dream their prayer was answered by a great river which came flowing out of a small spring. (Addition A:5–9, GNB)

The conclusion to the Greek version tells how this dream was fulfilled:

Then Mordecai said, "God has caused all these things to happen! And I am reminded of the dream I had about all of this. Every detail of the dream has come true. . . . The Lord saved his people! He rescued us from all these evils and performed great miracles and wonders that have never happened among other nations." (Addition F:1–7, GNB)

The Greek version adds a prayer of Mordecai, which uses language typical of mainstream Old Testament piety:

"O Lord, you are the Lord and King of all creation. . . . If you wish to save Israel, no one can stop you. You made heaven and earth and all the wonderful things on earth. . . . Long ago you chose us to be your people and rescued us from the land of Egypt. Do not abandon us now. We are your chosen people, so listen to my prayer and be gracious to us. . . . Save us from death so that we can keep on praising you. . . ." (Greek Esther, Addition C:2–10, GNB)

The Greek version also inserts a prayer of Esther, again in the typical language of Hebrew devotion, concluding, "Almighty God, listen to the prayer of your people. Rescue us from these evil men, and take away my fear." (Greek Esther, Addition C:30, GNB)

The effect of these Additions in the retelling of the story is to make explicit that which was only implicit in the Hebrew version: the role of God, and the importance of individual expressions of prayer and piety. In this Greek version, the story of Esther becomes another in the series of biblical stories which tell how God rescued his people.

But now, to the story itself.

How Esther Becomes Queen

The story begins with a look into the goings-on of the royal court in Susa. Xerxes, the king, had decided to make "a show of the riches of the imperial court with all its splendor and majesty" (Esther 1:4, GNB). He began, we are told, by inviting all of his officials and administrators to Susa for a six-month celebration. At the end of this period, the king threw a week-long party, to which he invited all of the men of the capital city, rich or poor. The detailed description gives evidence of the Jewish storyteller's fascination with such wealth and opulence:

> The courtyard there was decorated with blue and white cotton curtains, tied by cords of fine purple linen to silver rings on marble columns. Couches made of gold and silver had been placed in the courtyard, which was paved with white marble, red feldspar, shining mother-of-pearl, and blue turquoise. Drinks were served in gold cups, no two of them alike, and the king was generous with the royal wine. There were no limits on the drinks; the king had given orders to the palace servants that everyone could have as much as he wanted. (Esther 1:6–8, GNB)

During the course of this expensive stag party, the king ordered some of his staff to get his wife, Vashti, and to have her appear before the men so that he could show off her beauty, but Queen Vashti refused to come, and Xerxes became furious.

The king apparently did not know how to handle this minor domestic crisis. So he summoned some of his advisors and asked them what a king ought to do when his wife did not obey him. The advisors said:

> "Queen Vashti has insulted not only the king but also his officials—in fact, every man in the empire! Every woman in the empire will start looking down on her husband as soon as she hears what the queen has done. . . . When the wives of the royal officials of Persia and Media hear about the queen's behavior, they will be telling their husbands about it before the day is out. Wives everywhere will have no respect for their husbands, and husbands will be angry with their wives. If it please Your Majesty, issue a royal proclamation that Vashti may never again appear before the king. . . . Then give her place as queen to some better woman. When your proclamation is made known all over this huge empire, every woman will treat her husband with proper respect, whether he's rich or poor." (Esther 1:16–20, GNB)

The king took their advice, and Vashti was no longer queen. Then his advisors had yet another idea. They said:

> "Why don't you make a search to find some beautiful young virgins? You can appoint officials in every province of the empire and have them bring all these beautiful young girls to your harem here in Susa, the capital city . . . let them be given a beauty treatment. Then take the girl you like best and make her queen in Vashti's place." (Esther 2:2–4, GNB)

And so, in grand imperial style, a contest for "Miss Persia" was launched. Among the Jews living in Susa was a young girl named Esther, whose

Hebrew name was "Hadassah." (The reader will perhaps recall that the "Hadassah Society" is the name of a Jewish woman's organization; the "Hadassah Hospital" in Jerusalem also takes its name from this book of the Bible.) Esther's parents had died, and she was being brought up by her cousin, a man named Mordecai. She was, says the story, "a beautiful girl, and had a good figure" (Esther 2:7, GNB). Her beauty was noticed, and soon she was among the finalists in the royal contest. These finalists were given a special treatment, befitting the extravagance of the Persian court:

> The regular beauty treatment for the women lasted a year—massages with oil of myrrh for six months and with oil of balsam for six more. After that, each girl would be taken in turn to King Xerxes. When she went from the harem to the palace, she could wear whatever she wanted. She would go there in the evening, and the next morning she would be taken to another harem. . . . She would not go to the king again unless he liked her enough to ask for her by name. (Esther 2:12–14, GNB)

So Esther appeared before the king when her turn came, and it was Esther who was chosen to be the queen. However, upon the advice of her guardian Mordecai, she kept it a secret that she was Jewish.

She told the king about her cousin Mordecai, who was given an administrative position in the court. As he went about his duties, one day he heard two men plotting to kill the king. He told Esther, who warned the king, and the king's life was saved. Xerxes ordered that this information be recorded in the official records.

The Jewish Problem

To this point the story has moved along smoothly and rather quietly. The good Mordecai now has a job with the Persian government. Because of his alertness in averting a plot, his future seems secure. Esther, the poor orphan, has become Queen of Persia, and no one has any idea that the queen is Jewish.

Then Haman is introduced. The king appointed this man as prime minister and issued an order that all of the employees at the court were to bow down to him when he walked by. All did, except for one: Mordecai. When others asked him about this he explained, "I am a Jew, and I cannot bow to Haman" (Esther 3:4, GNB). The longer Greek version of Esther includes a prayer (note the mention of the Lord) which tells us why Mordecai would not bow to Haman:

"You know, Lord, that when I refused to bow to that arrogant Haman, it was
not because I was arrogant or trying to impress people. I simply did not want
to honor any man more than I honor you, my Lord. . . . If it would help to save
Israel, I would be willing even to kiss the soles of his feet." (Greek Esther,
Addition C:5–7, GNB)

Haman was furious when Mordecai would not bow to him. When he
found out that Mordecai was a Jew, he decided to deal with this problem by
initiating an order to kill all the Jews in the whole Persian empire. He said to
the king:

"There is a certain race of people scattered all over your empire and found in
every province. They observe customs that are not like those of any other people. Moreover, they do not obey the laws of the empire, so it is not in your best
interests to tolerate them. If it please Your Majesty, issue a decree that they are
to be put to death." (Esther 3:8–9, GNB)

The king approved of Haman's plan. The order went out through the whole
vast empire, saying that "on a single day, the thirteenth day of Adar, all Jews—
young and old, women and children—were to be killed. They were to be
slaughtered without mercy and their belongings were to be taken" (Esther
3:13, GNB).

Thus for the first time in history a decree is issued which deals with the
"Jewish problem" by ordering that all Jews be killed, simply because they are
Jews. The story of Esther presents us with the first proposal of a "pogrom" or
organized persecution of Jews. Here is the first recorded instance of an official
government policy of radical anti-Semitism.

When Mordecai learned of the proclamation, he joined the other Jews
throughout Persia in putting on sackcloth and covering himself with ashes, to
indicate great sorrow. Esther heard of her cousin's behavior and asked about
the reason. He told her about the plan to kill the Jews and asked her to
intercede with the king for the sake of her people. Esther told him that such
matters were not so easily done. Even the queen had to have special permission
to have an audience with the king, under the penalty of death if that permission were not granted! Mordecai sent her a message:

"Don't imagine that you are safer than any other Jew just because you are in
the royal palace. If you keep quiet at a time like this, help will come from
heaven to the Jews, and they will be saved, but you will die and your father's
family will come to an end. Yet who knows—maybe it was for a time like this
that you were made queen!" (Esther 4:13–14, GNB)

Esther sent word to Mordecai that all Jews should fast on her behalf. "After that," she said, "I will go to the king, even though it is against the law. If I must die for doing it, I will die." (4:16, GNB)

And so the tension in the story is at its maximum. Will the king hear Esther's request? And what will be his reaction?

Esther and Haman

The queen put on her robes and stood outside the throne room. When the king saw her, he held out his scepter, which meant that she had permission to enter. The first step had been successfully taken.

> "What is it, Queen Esther?" the king asked. "Tell me what you want, and you shall have it—even if it is half my empire." (Esther 5:3, GNB)

Esther told the king that she would like to invite him to a banquet, along with Prime Minister Haman. The king accepted the invitation, and the banquet took place that evening. After the meal, over the wine, the king asked again: "Tell me what you want, and you shall have it. I will grant your request, even if you ask for half my empire" (Esther 5:6, GNB).

This was the second time that the king had put this question to Esther. She makes her request:

> "If Your Majesty is kind enough to grant my request, I would like you and Haman to be my guests tomorrow at another banquet that I will prepare for you. At that time I will tell you what I want." (Esther 5:8, GNB)

Thus, we must wait for the third encounter between Esther and the king to see what she will request and how the king will react. The storyteller is effectively delaying the resolution of the tension. To keep us waiting a bit longer, he lets us watch Haman, as he leaves the banquet, where he had been the special guest of the king and the queen:

> When Haman left the banquet he was happy and in a good mood. But then he saw Mordecai at the entrance of the palace, and when Mordecai did not rise or show any sign of respect as he passed, Haman was furious with him. But he controlled himself and went on home. Then he invited his friends to his house and asked his wife Zeresh to join them. He boasted to them about how rich he was, how many sons he had, how the king had promoted him to high office, and how much more important he was than any of the king's other officials. "What is more," Haman went on, "Queen Esther gave a banquet for no one but the king and me, and we are invited back tomorrow. But none of

this means a thing to me as long as I see that Jew Mordecai sitting at the entrance of the palace." (Esther 5:9–13, GNB)

Then his wife and his friends made a suggestion to the prime minister:

"Why don't you have a gallows built, seventy-five feet tall? Tomorrow morning you can ask the king to have Mordecai hanged on it, and then you can go to the banquet happy."

Haman thought this was a good idea, so he had the gallows built. (Esther 5:14, GNB)

Another scene takes place, before we get to the banquet and hear the queen's request. The king had insomnia that night. Since he could not sleep, he asked one of his servants to read to him from the royal records. The servant happened to read the part which recorded how Mordecai had saved the king's life. The king said to his servants:

"How have we honored and awarded Mordecai for this?"

His servants answered, "Nothing has been done for him."

"Are any of my officials in the palace?" the king asked.

Now Haman had just entered the courtyard; he had come to ask the king to have Mordecai hanged on the gallows that was now ready. So the servants answered, "Haman is here, waiting to see you."

"Show him in," said the king.

So Haman came in, and the king said to him, "There is someone I wish very much to honor. What should I do for this man?"

Haman thought to himself, "Now who could the king want to honor so much? Me, of course."

So he answered the king, "Have royal robes brought for this man—robes that you yourself wear. Have a royal ornament put on your own horse. Then have one of your highest noblemen dress the man in these robes and lead him, mounted on the horse, through the city square. Have the nobleman announce as they go: 'See how the king rewards a man he wishes to honor!' "

Then the king said to Haman, "Hurry and get the robes and the horse, and provide these honors for Mordecai the Jew. Do everything for him that you have suggested. You will find him sitting at the entrance of the palace." (Esther 6:3–10, GNB)

Thus Haman receives the ultimate humiliation. He has to walk through the streets of the city of Susa, praising the one man in the world whom he despises!

Haman goes home that night and tells his wife and his friends of the day's happenings. Then we are prepared for the climax of the story as the king's servants come to pick up Haman for the banquet. The stage is set for Esther's third encounter with the king. Once again, the king says,

"Now, Queen Esther, what do you want? Tell me and you shall have it. I'll even give you half the empire."

Queen Esther answered, "If it please Your Majesty to grant my humble request, my wish is that I may live and that my people may live. My people and I have been sold for slaughter. If it were nothing more serious than being sold into slavery, I would have kept quiet and not bothered you about it; but we are about to be destroyed—exterminated!"

Then King Xerxes asked Queen Esther, "Who dares to do such a thing? Where is this man?"

Esther answered, "Our enemy, our persecutor, is this evil man Haman!"

Haman faced the king and queen with terror. The king got up in a fury, left the room, and went outside to the palace gardens. Haman could see that the king was determined to punish him for this, so he stayed behind to beg Queen Esther for his life. He had just thrown himself down on Esther's couch to beg for mercy, when the king came back into the room from the gardens. Seeing this, the king cried out, "Is this man going to rape the queen right here in front of me, in my own palace?"

The king had no sooner said this than the eunuchs covered Haman's head. Then one of them, who was named Harbonah, said, "Haman even went so far as to build a gallows at his house so that he could hang Mordecai, who saved Your Majesty's life. And it's seventy-five feet tall!"

"Hang Haman on it!" the king commanded.

So Haman was hanged on the gallows that he had built for Mordecai. Then the king's anger cooled down. (Esther 7:2–10, GNB)

From this point on, the action of the story begins to wind down. The decree from the king cannot be revoked, but he allows Mordecai to send out a proclamation stating that the Jews in all of the provinces of the empire will be allowed to organize and fight back. In the capital city, the Jews defeat five hundred of their enemies. The ten sons of Haman are hanged. In the provinces, the story tells us, some 75,000 enemies of the Jews are killed. And thus what began as Haman's final solution to the Jewish problem ends with the hanging of Haman and his sons, and the defeat of the enemies of the Jews.

For a New Time

What could this old story, which remains a part of Scripture for both the Jew and the Christian, mean for our time?

1. In the first place, it is clear that we miss the point of the story if we focus on the vengeance theme. The Bible itself provides a safeguard against this.[3] We have noted that the action of the story concludes with chapter 9, verse 16. Following this is material which indicates how the festival of Purim

is to be celebrated. The story is left as it stands, with its account of that gruesome slaughter of 75,000, but the emphasis of the festival is not on vengeance. Rather, Purim is to be "a time for feasting and giving gifts of food to one another" (Esther 9:19, GNB). The Jews were told "to observe these days with feasts and parties, giving gifts of food to one another and to the poor" (Esther 9:22, GNB). Purim, according to the biblical text itself, is to be a time to recall the joy of being delivered and then to share that joy with others, including the poor.

2. In Jewish communities throughout the world, the story is a familiar one because of its connection with the festival of Purim. Hermann Wouk describes a traditional Purim observance:

> Purim is Children's Night in the house of the Lord. It always has been, and the children sense their rights and exercise them. They carry flags and noisemakers, the traditional whirling rattles called "groggers," which can make a staggering racket. After the evening prayers the reading of the Book of Esther begins, solemnly enough, with the customary blessing over a scroll and the chanting of the opening verses in a special musical mode heard only on this holiday. The children are poised, waiting. The Reader chants through the first and second chapters and comes at last to the long-awaited sentence, "After these things, the king raised to power Haman the Agagite"—but nobody hears the last two words. The name "Haman" triggers off stamping, pounding, and a hurricane of groggers. The Reader waits patiently. The din dies. He chants on, and soon strikes another "Haman." Bedlam breaks loose again. This continues, and since Haman is now a chief figure in the story, the noisy outbursts come pretty frequently. The children, far from getting tired or bored, warm to the work. They do it with sure mob instinct: poised silence during the reading, explosions on each "Haman." Passages occur where Haman's name crops up several times in a very short space. The children's assaults come like pistol shots. The Reader's patience wears thin and finally breaks. It is impossible to read with so many interruptions. He gestures angrily at the children through the grogger storm and shoots a glance of appeal to the rabbi. This, of course, is what the children have been waiting for. The stag is down. Thereafter to the end it is a merciless battle between the Reader and the children. He tries to slur over the thick-falling "Hamans," they trip him every time with raucous salvos. He stumbles on to the final verse, exhausted, beaten, furious, and all is disordered hilarity in the synagogue. It is perhaps not quite fair to make the Reader stand in for Haman on this evening, but that is approximately what happens.[4]

I have witnessed a modern-day Purim celebration similar to that which Wouk describes, but with a technical addition to the festivities. At the front of the synagogue is mounted a full-sized traffic signal, with green, yellow, and red lights. When the name of Haman comes up during the reading of the story, the green light flashes, and the roar of groggers begins. Then, to attempt to give the hissing and the whirring of the groggers some sort of regulation, the light is switched to yellow and finally to red.

Other customs are associated with the modern celebration of Purim. *The Jewish Catalog* suggests the following:

> Write Haman's name on the bottom of your shoes and then kick and stamp. Bang together rocks with his name on them. Blow a shofar. Blow a trumpet. Play appropriate organ music. Play inappropriate organ music. Beat on a drum, pots and pans, etc. Shake a tin can full of nails (this can be devastating). Be imaginative. Use your head. There is also the custom to make a dummy Haman and beat it, hang it, burn it.[5]

3. In such a way the story of Esther is heard in the contemporary Jewish community, year by year, as the festival of Purim is celebrated. What could that story mean for the Christian community today?

We have noted that the book of Esther presents us with the earliest recorded instance of a mass program of anti-Semitism. Here we read the first account of a government-sponsored policy of genocide, of a horrible "final solution" for dealing with "the Jewish problem." For those of us living in this era after the Holocaust, Haman's decree has a familiar ring. He had said that "all Jews—young and old, women and children—were to be killed. They were to be slaughtered without mercy and their belongings were to be taken" (Esther 3:13 GNB). This sounds very much like the kind of pronouncements sent out under Hitler and the Nazi regime, which resulted in the Holocaust and the death of some six million Jews, including "young and old, women and children."

For those of us who are Christians, this story about Esther can remind us that we as Christians and as human beings can never again allow such anti-Semitism to flourish and erupt into the kind of madness that our generation has witnessed.

The most eloquent chronicler of the Holocaust events is Elie Wiesel, a Jew who was taken from his home at the age of fourteen and brought to the concentration camp at Auschwitz. He describes his first night there:

> Never shall I forget that night, the first night in camp, which has turned my life into one long night, seven times cursed and seven times sealed. Never shall I forget that smoke. Never shall I forget the little faces of the children, whose bodies I saw turned into wreaths of smoke beneath a silent blue sky.

Never shall I forget those flames which consumed my faith forever.

Never shall I forget that nocturnal silence which deprived me, for all eternity, of the desire to live. Never shall I forget those moments which murdered my God and my soul and turned my dreams to dust. Never shall I forget these things, even if I am condemned to live as long as God Himself. Never.[6]

How could these things have happened? This question has been asked time and again by thoughtful people of all faiths. Whatever the answer, one thing is clear: in this post-Holocaust era, the Christian community is obliged to take the initiative in seeking to understand its Jewish neighbors, so that the half-truths and distortions which lead to anti-Semitism and which led to the Holocaust cannot be perpetuated.

The Christian and Jewish communities have lived alongside one another for almost two thousand years now. For most of that time there has been little contact between the two. For millions of Christians, the word "Jew" only conjures up stereotypes which should have been eradicated by genuine conversation and enlightened understanding long ago.

In this time after the Holocaust, the book of Esther could call us to a new conversation with one another. Christians could visit a Purim celebration and then discuss with Jewish neighbors what it was that allowed a Haman, or a Hitler, to come to power.

For our time, this old story is a call to dialogue between Christians and Jews.

And who knows—maybe it was for a time like this that the story of Esther was made a part of the Bible, for Jews, but especially for Christians, too.

CHAPTER 8

Amazing Grace

Jonah

Imagine that you are taking a word-association test. You are asked to give the first thing that comes to your mind, when you hear each of the following: "Romeo and _____ . . . bacon and _____ . . . Jonah and _____." Chances are that your responses would be "Juliet," "eggs," and "the whale." The book of Jonah has been "tied to the tale of a whale," one suspects, ever since the story was first told, and, of course, it is that huge fish which makes the story unique and exciting.

But as we look at this old story more closely we discover that the "fish" is mentioned in only three of the forty-eight verses of the book (1:17; 2:1; 2:10). Although this is less than ten percent of the story, we could safely suggest that the fish has occupied more than ninety percent of the discussion about this prophetic book.

What is the message of the book of Jonah? Luther once wrote: "This is an exceptionally wonderful story. Even Christ seems to have been delighted with it."[1]

And later he said "[Jonah] represents an excellent, outstanding, and comforting example of faith and a mighty and wonderful sign of God's goodness to all the world."[2]

The story is indeed an "exceptionally wonderful" one. It must have been well-known during the first century A.D. since Jesus refers to it in a way that assumes his hearers know it (Matt. 12:38–41). And while he focused on the incident with the whale, he also made mention of the people of Nineveh, those non-Israelites who repented. It may be that this hint can point us in the direction of understanding this old story for our time, as "a mighty and wonderful sign of God's goodness to all the world."

Some Preliminaries

The setting for the action of the story is clear. "Jonah son of Amittai" is known from 2 Kings 14:25. There he appears as a prophet who lived during the eighth century B.C., when Jeroboam was king of Israel (786–746 B.C.). Just after the death of Jeroboam, the Assyrian empire enjoyed a revival. By 722 B.C. they had pushed over into the west and captured Samaria, the capital of the northern kingdom. When Sennacherib became emperor in 704 B.C., he made Nineveh the capital and thus the most powerful city in the world of its day.

But what of the setting for the composition of the story? Once again this question is difficult to answer with certainty. Obviously, the earliest possible date would be sometime during the eighth century. The latest would have to be before the date of the composition of the book of Sirach in the second century B.C. There we read, "May the bones of the twelve prophets rise to new life . . ." (Sirach 49:10, GNB), which is a reference to the "Book of the Twelve" or the Minor Prophets of which the book of Jonah is a part.

Because the language of the book fits best into the post-exilic period, and because the storyteller seems to be remembering Nineveh as he had heard about it, a Nineveh of the far distant past (there was no "king" of Nineveh; the size of the city is exaggerated in 3:3) the book appears to have been composed sometime during the Persian period (539–332 B.C.). During this time the Jews were a very small island in the midst of the vast sea of the Persian empire. They were but a tiny remnant of the people of God trying to make their way in the midst of the peoples of the world.

1. What was the situation of the people of God during these years after the exile? In 538 B.C., Cyrus, the King of Persia, issued an edict to the Jewish people in his realm. It said, "You are to go to Jerusalem and rebuild the Temple of the LORD, the God of Israel, the God who is worshiped in Jerusalem" (Ezra 1:3, GNB). The Persians even promised to provide government grants to aid in the project (Ezra 6:4).

Some of the Jews who had been living in captivity in Babylon returned to Jerusalem. Others preferred to remain in Babylon, but supported the venture with their money (Ezra 1:4). Thus, after a long period living away from their land, the Jews began to return to build up Jerusalem and their homeland.

The book of Ezra tells us about the rebuilding of the temple, or the construction of the "second temple" as it has come to be called. The foundations were laid, and there was a celebration. However, the joy was bittersweet, when some of the older people who could remember Solomon's temple saw this newer, less magnificent structure:

> Everyone shouted with all his might, praising the LORD, because the work on the foundation of the Temple had been started. Many of the older priests, Levites, and heads of clans had seen the first Temple, and as they watched the foundation of this Temple being laid, they cried and wailed. But the others who were there shouted for joy. No one could distinguish between the joyful shouts and the crying, because the noise they made was so loud that it could be heard for miles. (Ezra 3:11–13, GNB)

Life back in the homeland was not pleasant. Living conditions were primitive, neighbors were hostile, and before long, work on the temple ground to a halt. The morale of the community sank to a dangerously low point.

Around the year 520 B.C., some eighteen years after the Jews had begun to return to resettle Jerusalem, the prophet Haggai appeared on the scene. He had one mission in mind: to get the temple built and thereby aid in reviving the spirit of the small community of the people of God. He said, speaking in the name of the Lord:

> "My people, why should you be living in well-built houses while my Temple lies in ruins? Don't you see what is happening to you? You have planted much grain, but have harvested very little. You have food to eat, but not enough to make you full. You have wine to drink, but not enough to get drunk on! You have clothing, but not enough to keep you warm. And the working man cannot earn enough to live on. Can't you see why this has happened? Now go up into the hills, get lumber, and rebuild the Temple; then I will be pleased and will be worshiped as I should be." (Hag. 1:4–8, GNB)

The temple did get built and was dedicated in 515 B.C. There were even hopes that since the temple was finished, God would shake the heavens and the earth and the Messiah would come (Hag. 2:20–23), but no such thing happened. No Messiah appeared, and life went on.

The spirit of the small post-exilic community sank even lower. As evidence for the mood during the years between about 500–450 B.C., we have the collected preaching of the prophet Malachi, the last of the books in our Old Testament. As we listen to these words, we discover that the clergy at the time are bored with their work and offer sick animals for sacrifices (Mal. 1:6–13). The religious leaders have failed to offer correct instruction (Mal. 2:8). Divorce has become a scandal in the community (Mal. 2:13–16). Evil is tolerated, so that the lives of the people of God look no different from the lives of the people of the world (2:17). People cheat on their tithes (3:8–10), saying that religion doesn't pay, and that evil doers are actually better off (3:13–15). And the Lord, says the prophet, is tired of the cynical, pseudo-theological talk of this people (2:17). Judging from the situation as we infer it from careful listening to the preaching of this prophet, it seems that the people of God were dangerously near the point of assimilation. It could well have happened that they would have disappeared as a people, simply blending in with the peoples who lived around them.

2. After the time of Malachi, in the second half of the fifth century B.C., we encounter two individuals who did much to save the post-exilic community from assimilation and to shape the future of Judaism in the years following. The first was Nehemiah, a Jew who had become an official in the Persian court, and who succeeded in giving the small community political security.

While going about his work in Persia, he learned of the sad state of his people in Judah and asked permission to travel there to help in rebuilding Jerusalem. The Persian emperor gave him such permission, even granting him a supply of timber, and Nehemiah set out for Judah. After making a secret inspection of the city at night (Neh. 2:11–15) he said to his fellow Jews, "See what trouble we are in because Jerusalem is in ruins and its gates are destroyed! Let's rebuild the city walls and put an end to our disgrace" (Neh. 2:17, GNB). Despite formidable opposition from hostile neighbors, which necessitated working with one hand and keeping a weapon in the other (Neh. 4:16–21), Nehemiah got the wall finished in less than two months time (Neh. 6:15). In this way, the people of God were given political security, now surrounded by the wall which protected them from the hostile peoples surrounding them.

The other individual who provided leadership during this period was Ezra. Though the details of his relationship to Nehemiah are not clear, it appears that he arrived some time after Nehemiah had begun his work. If Nehemiah rebuilt the wall and gave the people political security, it was Ezra who revitalized the law, reminding them of their religious identity and giving them religious security. In reading the books of Nehemiah and Ezra we discover that at this time the Sabbath was being neglected (Neh. 13:15–18). Many Jews had married outside the faith, thus accelerating the trend toward assimilation (Neh. 13:23–27). The children were not being instructed in Hebrew. As they forgot the language of their people and of worship, there was a danger that they would forget their religion as well (Neh. 13:24–25).

Thus Ezra, with Nehemiah's support, took some drastic measures to get religion going again. The problem of mixed marriages had to be dealt with. Preaching a sermon to a crowd standing out in the rain, Ezra told them to send their foreign wives away, along with any children born to the marriages (Ezra 10). The Sabbath was enforced (Neh. 13:19–22). Nehemiah had surrounded the people with a wall; now Ezra marked off the boundaries between the people of God and the peoples of the world by surrounding them with the fence of the law.

Such measures seem intolerant and unreasonably narrow-minded, to our modern ears, but let it be said that without this insistence upon taking the religion of Israel with utmost concern, Judaism would no doubt have gone under. As intermarriage went on, as one observance after another was dropped, a total assimilation would have taken place. Nehemiah and Ezra were God's men for that particular hour in their nation's history.

3. As the years of the post-exilic period went on, however, the separatism which had been such a necessity at the time of Nehemiah and Ezra developed into an unhealthy exclusivism. Such marks of their religion as dietary laws, Sabbath observance, marriage regulations, circumcision, and the continued use of Hebrew in worship set the people of God apart from the peoples in whose midst they lived. In studying this period, one cannot escape the feeling that along with a certain pride in being "insiders" who were recipients of God's grace, there developed among the people of God an attitude of suspicion and prejudice toward the Gentiles, the "outsiders" who lived in the world surrounding them. It was to this community which was in danger of turning in upon itself and forgetting its calling to be a "light to the nations" (Isa. 49:6) that the story of Jonah was first addressed.

The Story

The book of Jonah is unique among the prophetic books of the Bible in two ways. First, it is the only prophetic book which consists entirely of a story about a prophet. Other prophetic books contain narrative materials (Isa. 36–

39; Amos 7:10–17), but the books are mainly collections of prophetic sayings. Secondly, Jonah is the only prophet who is told to go and preach in a city not in the territory of Israel or Judah. While other prophetic books contain collections of sayings concerning foreign nations (Amos 1–2; Isa. 13–23), these prophets spoke their words in the land of Israel or Judah.

   1. The first scene (1:1–3) presents us with language typical of a prophet receiving a word from God. We are told of Elijah, "Then the word of the LORD came to him, 'Arise, go to Zarephath . . .' " (1 Kings 17:8–9). Jeremiah reports, "And the word of the LORD came to me, saying . . ." (Jer. 1:11). The book of Jonah begins, "Now the word of the LORD came to Jonah the son of Amittai, saying, 'Arise, go to Nineveh . . .' " (1:1–2).

   Nineveh. If we are to understand this story, we must begin by learning something about Nineveh. Located on the Tigris River, more than five hundred miles to the northeast of the land of Israel, Nineveh was the capital of the Assyrian empire during its heyday in the eighth and seventh centuries B.C. For the Jew living in the post-exilic period, to whom the story of Jonah was first addressed, Nineveh was remembered as a symbol of all that was despised in the enemies of the people of God. In 722 B.C., the Assyrians had conquered Samaria, the capital of the northern kingdom. The inhabitants had been deported and foreigners had been imported in their place (2 Kings 17), but little more than a century later, in 612 B.C., Nineveh fell to the armies of the Medes and Babylonians, and the Assyrian empire came to an end. The prophet Nahum announced its doom. In listening to the way in which he speaks about that city, we can catch something of the attitude of the Jews and of others who had lived under the rule of the Assyrians:

> Doomed is the lying, murderous city,
>   full of wealth to be looted and plundered! . . .
> Nineveh the whore is being punished.
> Attractive and full of deadly charms,
>   she enchanted nations and enslaved them.
> The LORD Almighty says,
>   "I will punish you, Nineveh!
>   I will strip you naked and let the nations see you,
>   see you in all your shame.
> I will treat you with contempt
>   and cover you with filth.
>   People will stare at you in horror.
> All who see you will shrink back.

They will say, 'Nineveh lies in ruins!
Who has any sympathy for her?
Who will want to comfort her?' " (Nah. 3:1–7, GNB)

And then, in the final words of that prophet, is reflected the attitude of those who had felt the pain of Assyrian oppression:

> All those who hear the news of your destruction clap their hands for joy. Did anyone escape your endless cruelty? (Nah. 3:19, GNB)

As late as Tobit, a story in the Apocrypha written in the second century B.C., the reputation of Nineveh remains:

> "Tobias, my son, leave Nineveh now. Do not stay here . . . . It is a wicked city and full of immorality; the people here have no sense of shame." (Tobit 14:10, GNB)

"Go to Nineveh, that great city." Why would God want to send a prophet to *that* place? This would be the question of any pious Jew hearing the story about Jonah. It would be as if a Jew who had been through the death camps were told, "Arise, go to Germany." Or an American who had been touched by the Iranian treatment of hostages in 1980, "Arise, go to Teheran." With this command to the prophet at the beginning of the story, one thing is clear. God cares about the city of Nineveh. He cares about the very people that his own chosen people disliked the most. He cares, and he wants to send a prophet to them.

The prophet Jonah does not share the Lord's concern for that city full of Assyrians. Told to go east, he catches the next ship heading west. "He paid his fare and went aboard with the crew to sail to Spain, where he would be away from the LORD" (Jon.1:3, GNB). Thus the tension of the story is introduced: what will happen to a prophet who tries to run away from the task God has given him?

2. In reading the story of Ruth, we noted that the narrator mentioned the Lord only two times, at the beginning and the end of the story (Ruth 1:6 and 4:13). In the book of Esther, God's name did not appear at all. But Jonah is quite different. At each crucial point of the story, it is the Lord who acts. At the beginning of the second scene (Jon. 1:4–16), on board a ship headed for Spain, we are told that, "the LORD sent a strong wind on the sea, and the storm was so violent that the ship was in danger of breaking up" (Jon. 1:4, GNB). This ship was manned by sailors who were, like the Assyrians, not a part of God's chosen people, but representatives of the people of the world. What

would these pagan sailors do when there was a storm? We are told, "The sailors were terrified and cried out for help, each one to his own god. Then, in order to lessen the danger, they threw the cargo overboard" (Jon. 1:5, GNB). When these people of the world are in trouble, they do two things: they pray, and then they go into action.

What of our man Jonah? He, we should remember, is the representative of *our* community, the people of God, on board that ship. "Meanwhile, Jonah had gone below and was lying in the ship's hold, sound asleep" (Jon. 1:5, GNB). At this point in the story, the "worldly" sailors look much better than Jonah!

The captain comes upon Jonah and rouses him. He is a pious man, like most seafaring folk, and first of all he urges Jonah to pray! The sailors, who now fear for their lives, understand the crisis theologically. They suspect that this terrible storm must be a punishment from the gods. Perhaps there is a criminal on board! So they draw straws to discover who the guilty one might be, and it is Jonah who gets the short straw.

They question this stranger: "What are you doing here? What country do you come from? What is your nationality?" (Jon. 1:8, GNB). Jonah answers, and identifies himself as a man of piety: "I am a Hebrew. . . . I worship the LORD, the God of heaven who made land and sea" (Jon. 1:9, GNB). He goes on to explain that he is running away from this Lord. If they will but throw him into the sea, he continues, the storm will cease. But once again these pagan sailors prove to be men of rather extraordinary good will. They struggle against the storm, pulling at the oars, risking their lives to try to get the ship to shore. But they can make no headway at all. When the storm continues to worsen, they pray to Jonah's God:

> "O LORD, we pray, don't punish us with death for taking this man's life! You, O LORD, are responsible for all this; it is your doing." (Jon. 1:14, GNB)

They take Jonah, throw him overboard, and the storm ceases. The sea calms down at once. Seeing this miracle, the sailors worship the Lord, offer a sacrifice, and promise to serve him!

Thus Jonah, who was reluctant to preach to the pagans in Nineveh, ends up becoming an unusual but effective witness to his Lord. The sailors all become worshipers of the God of Jonah. What happens when a prophet tries to run away from the task God has given him? God sees to it that the job gets done anyway. The prophet has become a successful missionary, despite himself!

3. Scene one was initiated by the word of the Lord coming to Jonah (Jon.

1:1). Scene two began when "the LORD sent a strong wind" (Jon. 1:4). The third scene (Jon. 1:17–2:10) is again introduced by an act of God: "And the LORD appointed a great fish to swallow up Jonah" (Jon. 1:17). Jonah had said that the Lord was "the God of heaven, who made land and sea" (Jon. 1:9, GNB). Now the story tells us more about the nature of this God: he can "appoint" a huge fish (Jon. 1:17), or a plant (Jon. 4:6) or a worm (Jon. 4:7). This God has created, and he can also intervene in the processes of the sea and land, as he wishes!

The situation in this third scene is a somewhat comical one. We might imagine the prophet waking, shaking himself, and then being amazed to discover that he is cruising through the Mediterranean, seated comfortably inside a huge fish! He realizes that he has been rescued from drowning, and can only react with a song of praise to the Lord! The poet Aldous Huxley has caught the scene well:

> Seated upon the convex mound
> Of one vast kidney, Jonah prays,
> And sings his canticles and hymns,
> Making the hollow vault resound
> God's goodness and mysterious ways,
> Till the great fish spouts music as he swims.[3]

The scene had begun with an act of God. It ends with God acting once again, "Then the LORD ordered the fish to spit Jonah up on the beach, and it did" (Jon. 2:10, GNB). And so there he sits, in the sunshine. The fish was no doubt as glad to be rid of his unexpected cargo as Jonah was to be freed from his unusual submarinal conveyance!

4. In the Hebrew Bible, the first words of the fourth scene are identical with these of the beginning of the book: "Then the word of the LORD came to Jonah." We are, the story indicates, right back where we started. In terms of the question which expresses the tension of the story, we see what happens when a prophet tries to run away from a task which God wants done: after a series of experiences which can only be described as highly unusual, God gives the prophet another chance! Once again he is told, "Arise, go to Nineveh, that great city, and proclaim to it the message that I tell you" (Jon. 3:2).

This time Jonah does set out for Nineveh. He goes part way into the city, without much enthusiasm it would seem, and says, "In forty days Nineveh will be destroyed!" (Jon. 3:4, GNB).

This city, we recall, was remembered by the hearers of the story of Jonah as among the worst in the world. They thought of it as populated by heathen, pagan, children of the world, who had been the oppressors of God's own people. And how will these pagans react to the preaching of this prophet from Israel?

> The people of Nineveh believed God's message. So they decided that everyone should fast, and all the people, from the greatest to the least, put on sackcloth to show that they had repented. (Jon. 3:5, GNB)

The king himself sent out the decree, "All persons and animals must wear sackcloth. Everyone must pray earnestly to God and must give up his wicked behavior and his evil actions" (Jon. 3:8, GNB).

An interesting detail in the story: all of Nineveh repents, from king to people and even to the animals (Jon. 3:8)! Here we see a conception of the relationship between human beings and the animals which did not yet make the sharp break between them, such as is characteristic of our own time. Humans and animals are all viewed as part of the same family of creatures on the earth. This statement, along with the last verse of the story of Jonah, sounds quite modern in our day when we are rediscovering the fact that we are all part of one ecological family traveling together on "spaceship earth." It could also speak a word in the context of the renewed discussion about evolution, where believing people are often reluctant to acknowledge any kinship with the other creatures of the earth!

The whole of the huge city of Nineveh repents. And what does God do? He changes his mind, and decides not to destroy the city after all.

5. The last scene in the story presents us with a dialogue between Jonah and the Lord. (Again, we note the difference between this story and those of Ruth and Esther, which contained no such direct communication between God and people.) Despite his half-hearted efforts, Jonah has become a successful evangelist. In fact, the entire city took his message to heart! They repented, and God has spared them from destruction.

How would a preacher react to such results? How would an evangelist feel, after conducting a campaign in a huge city and having the entire population repent and pledge to change its ways? Any such person would praise the Lord and be delighted, one would think. But Jonah? He says:

> "LORD, didn't I say before I left home that this is just what you would do? That's why I did my best to run away to Spain! I knew that you are a loving and merciful God, always patient, always kind, and always ready to change your

mind and not punish. Now then, LORD let me die. I am better off dead than alive." (Jon. 4:2–3, GNB)

Jonah knows his Bible. His statement sounds almost like a creed ("He is kind and full of mercy; he is patient and keeps his promise," Joel 2:13, GNB; cf. Exod. 34:6). And now we discover an unpleasant side to the prophet's personality. Now we learn why he did not go to Nineveh in the first place. He knew what God was like and was afraid that something like this might happen! God just might call off the destruction! Jonah wanted those pagan Ninevites to get what (he thought) they had coming to them, but now God has changed his mind. If the Assyrians are "in" with the people of God, then Jonah wants out! He wants out badly enough to die.

God asks, "Do you do well to be angry?" (Jon. 4:4).

Then Jonah sits down someplace east of the city and looks at it. He wonders if these wicked, worldly people are really going to get by without being punished.

Then God acts again. The same God who had "appointed" the fish now "appoints" a plant, which immediately grows up and gives Jonah some shade. The prophet is delighted with this minor miracle. But the next day God does some more "appointing." This time it is a worm, which attacks the plant, which then withers and dies. Once again Jonah is angry, angry enough to die.

God asks again, "Do you do well to be angry for the plant?" (Jon. 4:9). Jonah defends his anger. Then God uses the "from minor to major" argument which is familiar in the biblical tradition. This argument is usually marked by the expression, "how much more;" Jesus used it (Matt. 7:11; Luke 12:24; 12:28) as did Paul (Rom. 11:12). Here the thought is, "Jonah, you care about what happens to this plant. It was here just yesterday and now has died. You did nothing for it. If you care that much about a plant, don't you think that I care about a whole city full of people?"

But God's care does not extend only to the people. Once again, we hear about the animals in Nineveh:

> "And should not I pity Nineveh, that great city, in which there are more than a hundred and twenty thousand persons who do not know their right hand from their left, and also much cattle?" (Jon. 4:11)

What happens to a prophet who tries to run away from the task God has asked him to do? In this case, the story ends with a question addressed to the prophet.

And now you, who have just heard the story, are left to answer it. Shouldn't God care for the city, that Gentile city, teeming with thousands of people? Shouldn't he also care for those cattle, those gentle cattle, grazing on an Assyrian hillside?

For a New Time

Jonah was a prophet who lived in the eighth century B.C. The story about his adventures was told for a new time centuries later, during the post-exilic period, but what word might this story have for our time?

The first question to be considered when reflecting on this story is: "Who is Jonah?" Our first answer might be, "Jonah? Why, Jonah, of course, is Israel. Jonah is the people of God of the post-exilic period, a people who had turned in upon themselves and who had forgotten their calling to be a 'light to the nations.' " That answer would be true. The story did speak a word to such a people in the time after the exile. But if we read the Bible as Scripture, expecting also a word from God for our time, then we can't rest with that answer.

Who is Jonah? We might answer by saying, "Jonah is the church. Here is a word addressed to a people of God which has become self-centered, more interested in nourishing its own programs than in caring for the hurts of the world." Once again, the answer would be a correct one. Since the tendency of the church is always to turn our backs on the "outsiders" and focus our concern on our own community, the word of Jonah is one which the church needs to hear, which disturbs us out of our complacency, and calls us to our task.

Who is Jonah?

As we continue to reflect on that question we notice that the story ends with a question directed to an individual. That question is directed to one, single person who knows all the pious language (Jon. 1:8–9), who can list the attributes of God (Jon. 4:2), and who is definitely an insider, one of God's people. However, there is something wrong with the person to whom that question is addressed. Despite an apparently God-fearing upbringing, that person does *not* pity Nineveh and does *not* care about those living there. Though the one to whom the question is addressed knows that God is "a gracious God and merciful, slow to anger, and abounding in steadfast love" (Jon. 4:2), he cannot bear to think of that steadfast love being extended to *those* people! This is the same attitude which we find in stories Jesus told. There stands the elder son, sulking and refusing to join the party when his rebellious brother came home (Luke 15:25–32). There are those "insiders" who grumble and begrudge the generosity of a God who would welcome "outsiders" to come in and become a part of God's people after a life lived apart from that people (Matt. 20:1–16).

Who is Jonah? When I listen to that story carefully, I discover that the question with which the story ends is directed to an individual, and that individual *is me*! When I hear the story rightly, I see myself in that pious, theologically educated runaway who is huddled in the hold of the ship while the "pagans" on board are out in the storm struggling to save the lives of everyone, my own included! I also have to identify with that child of God who knows all the right religious responses but who sits sulking and sorrowing because God cares for some people whom I have always considered not worthy of his love.

2. Thus the first word which this old story has for our time is a negative one. It is a word against exclusivism, against prejudice toward the "outsider" on the part of those who believe themselves to be "insiders" with something of a monopoly on God's grace.

Imagine for a moment a football game, played in one of the great sports arenas of the land. The sky is clear, the stands are packed, the grass is fresh and green. The kick-off, the ball is received, and is run back. Then the offensive team prepares for the first play. There they are, trained, disciplined, equipped for the game. They go into the huddle. The crowd is expectant, but then a strange thing happens: the team stays in the huddle. When the referee goes out to investigate, the team refuses to come out of the huddle! They believe that their whole purpose is huddling! They think that they have been trained, disciplined, and equipped *to huddle*.

Now that is a ridiculous picture, but consider for a moment the fact that week by week, God's people gather into "huddles" all over the world. That gathering, that huddling, is very important for the life of those people, but it is not by any means the sole purpose of their existence as people of God. The huddling, the gathering for worship, is a time to be reminded of the good news and to be inspired to break out of the huddle and go back into the world as witnesses to that good news, in words and acts of care for the people of the world.

3. And thus this "exceptionally wonderful story" conveys a positive word, too. It is a "mighty and wonderful sign of God's goodness to all the world." That positive word is summarized in the words of Jonah himself: "I knew that thou art a gracious God and merciful, slow to anger, and abounding in steadfast love" (Jon. 4:2).

In the home where I grew up there was a picture of Jesus sitting on a hill, looking over the city of Jerusalem. The caption under the painting read, "O Jerusalem, Jerusalem . . . how often would I have gathered thy children together, even as a hen gathereth her chickens under *her* wings, and ye would not!" (Matt. 23:37, KJV). Jesus cared for the city of Jerusalem. The story of Jonah reminds us of God's care for the other cities of the world, for the Ninevehs and Calcuttas, the Moscows and Chicagos, filled with hundreds of thousands of people "who do not know their right hand from their left."

This story reaches out to that story told in the Gospels and summarized in the words of Jesus: "For God so loved the world [all the peoples of the world] that he gave his only Son, that whoever believes in him should not perish but have eternal life" (John 3:16). The same thing is said in the words of a song which children still sing in Sunday schools across the land, "Red and yellow, black and white, They are precious in his sight; Jesus loves the little children of the world."

The word about God's amazing grace which this story conveys is not only a general one about God's love for the whole world, it is also individualized. The last phrase in the story of Jonah is, "and also much cattle." God cares even about the cows grazing on the hillsides of Assyria. To apply the "minor to major" argument: if God cares about the cows of Nineveh, don't you think he cares about you? Jesus once expressed a similar idea, though he spoke about sparrows instead of cows (Matt. 10:29–31). The old Gospel song paraphrased his words, "His eye's upon the sparrow, and I know he watches me." The message of those final words of our story could be summarized, "His eye's upon the cows of Nineveh—and I know he watches me!"

4. Finally, if we have listened carefully, this old story about God's grace leaves us with a task. If it is true that God cares about the people of the world, and if we are a people who know that and who have enjoyed living as a part of his people, then it becomes clear that our task is the same as that of Jonah. The

word of the Lord once came to him, saying, "Rise, go to Nineveh." That was a word directed to one individual.

Another word has been directed to the Lord's church:

> "Go, then, to all peoples everywhere and make them my disciples: baptize them in the name of the Father, the Son, and the Holy Spirit, and teach them to obey everything I have commanded you. And I will be with you always, to the end of the age." (Matt. 28:19–20, GNB)

Years after the time of Jonah, God's amazing grace was personified in Jesus, the Messiah, and the "go" which was once directed to one individual, sending him to one city, has now been directed to a whole people, sending them out into the whole world: "Go, then," said Jesus, not just to Nineveh, but "to all peoples, everywhere."

With such a concern, it is not surprising that Jesus found delight in the story of Jonah.

NOTES

CHAPTER 1: "A TIME FOR STORIES"

1. Hans Küng, *On Being a Christian*, translated by Edward Quinn (Garden City: Doubleday & Company, 1976), p. 52.

2. *Minneapolis Tribune*, July 2, 1978, p. 6D. Reprinted with permission from the *Minneapolis Tribune*.

3. *Time*, Sept. 18, 1978, p. 100. Copyright 1978 Time Inc. Reprinted by permission from TIME.

4. *Time*, Aug. 3, 1981, p. 6. Copyright 1981 Time Inc. Reprinted by permission from TIME.

5. Claus Westermann, *Elements of Old Testament Theology*, translated by Douglas W. Stott (Atlanta: John Knox Press, 1982), p. 9.

6. Ibid., p. 11.

7. Ibid., p. 11.

8. "A Declaration of Faith," *The Proposed Book of Confessions of the Presbyterian Church in the United States* (Atlanta: Stated Clerk of the General Assembly of the Presbyterian Church in the United States, 1974), p. 145. Reprinted by permission.

9. Robert M. Herhold, "Conversation with Sittler," *LCA Partners* (June 1979), p. 8. Reprinted by permission.

10. From THE GATES OF THE FOREST by Elie Wiesel. Translated by Frances Frenaye. Copyright © 1966 by Holt, Rinehart and Winston. Reprinted by permission of Holt, Rinehart and Winston, Publishers. Pp. 6-10, Bard Books, published by Avon.

CHAPTER 2: "LISTENING TO THE STORIES"

1. Martin Buber, *Tales of the Hasidim: The Early Masters* (New York: Schocken Books, 1947), pp. v-vi.

2. *"Was ist eine Erzählung? Eine Erzählung dichtet ein Geschehen von einer Spannung zu einer Lösung."* Claus Westermann, *Genesis, Biblischer Kommentar* I/2 (Neukirchen-Vluyn: Neukirchener Verlag des Erziehungsvereins, 1977), p. 33. Reprinted by permission.

3. Jacob Licht, *Storytelling in the Bible* (Jerusalem: The Magnes Press, The Hebrew University, 1978), pp. 96-98.

4. Ibid., p. 11. Reprinted by permission.

5. Elie Wiesel, *Messengers of God*, translated from the French by Marion Wiesel (New York: Random House, 1976), pp. 69-97.

6. Claus Westermann, *Genesis*, I/2, p. 447.

CHAPTER 3: "MATCHMAKER, MATCHMAKER" (Genesis 24)

1. Reprinted from FIDDLER ON THE ROOF. Copyright © 1964 by Joseph Stein. Used by permission of Crown Publishers, Inc.

2. On the biblical theme of blessing, see Claus Westermann, *Blessing in the Bible and the Life of the Church*, translated by Keith Crim (Philadelphia: Fortress Press, 1978).

3. Claus Westermann, *God's Angels Need No Wings*, translated by David L. Scheidt (Philadelphia: Fortress Press, 1979), pp. 104-105. Reprinted by permission of Fortress Press.

CHAPTER 4: "GOD IS WORKING HIS PURPOSE OUT: Purpose Irregular" (Genesis 37-50)

1. *The New Yorker*, Jan. 24, 1977, p. 88.

2. James B. Pritchard, editor, *Ancient Near Eastern Texts*, 2nd edition (Princeton: Princeton University Press, 1955), p. 414.

3. See the discussion in John Bright, *A History of Israel*, 3rd edition (Philadelphia: Westminster Press, 1981), pp. 59-61, 87.

4. See the discussion in Claus Westermann, *Genesis* I/3, pp. 4-12.

5. Gerhard von Rad, "The Joseph Narrative and Ancient Wisdom," *The Problem of the Hexateuch and Other Essays*, translated by E.W. Trueman Dicken (New York: McGraw-Hill Book Company, 1966), pp. 292-300.

6. Ibid., pp. 294-295.

7. Claus Westermann, *A Thousand Years and a Day*, translated by Stanley Rudman (Philadelphia: Muhlenberg Press, 1962), p. 49. Reprinted by permission of Fortress Press.

8. Gerhard von Rad, *Genesis*, translated by John H. Marks (Philadelphia: The Westminster Press, 1961), p. 371.

9. Martin Luther, *Lectures on Genesis*, translated by Paul D. Pahl, pp. 321-322. FROM: LUTHER'S WORKS. Volume 7. © 1965 Concordia Publishing House. Used by permission.

10. Gerhard von Rad, *Genesis*, p. 393.

11. Claus Westermann, "Die Joseph-Erzählung," in *Calwer Predigthilfen*, Band 5 (Stuttgart: Calwer Verlag, 1966), p. 114; my translation.

12. Ibid., p. 25, my translation.

13. Westermann, *A Thousand Years and a Day*, p. 49.

CHAPTER 5: "TALES FROM THE WILD, WILD WEST BANK" (Judges 6–8, 13–16)

1. Westermann, *A Thousand Years and a Day*, p. 103.

2. See the discussion on p. 6, chapter 1 above.

3. Bright, p. 180.

4. Martin Luther, *Table Talk*, edited and translated by Theodore G. Tappert, *Luther's Works*, vol. 54 (Philadelphia: Fortress Press, 1967), p. 79. Reprinted by permission of Fortress Press.

5. Bernhard W. Anderson, UNDERSTANDING THE OLD TESTAMENT, 3rd ed., © 1975, p. 154. Reprinted by permission of Prentice-Hall, Inc., Englewood Cliffs, N.J.

6. B. Davie Napier, *Song of the Vineyard* (New York: Harper & Brothers, 1962), p. 144.

7. Frederick Manfred, *Lord Grizzly* (New York: New American Library, 1954), p. 9.

8. Bright, p. 185.

CHAPTER 6: "TWO LOVE STORIES" (Ruth)

1. Cf. the perceptive comments of Ronald M. Hals in *The Theology of the Book of Ruth*, Facet Books, Biblical Series 23 (Philadelphia: Fortress Press, 1969), pp. 3ff.

2. Phyllis Trible, *God and the Rhetoric of Sexuality* (Philadelphia: Fortress Press, 1978), p. 173; Chapter 6 was previously published in *Soundings* 59 (Fall 1976): 251-79. Copyright 1976, The Society for Religion in Higher Education and Vanderbilt University.

3. Frederick Buechner, *Peculiar Treasures* (San Francisco: Harper & Row, 1979), p. 148.

4. Ibid., pp. 148-149.

5. C. C. McCown, "City," in *The Interpreter's Dictionary of the Bible,* edited by George Arthur Buttrick, vol. 1 (Nashville: Abingdon Press, 1962), p. 634.

6. Edward F. Campbell, Jr., *Ruth, The Anchor Bible,* vol. 7 (Garden City: Doubleday & Company, 1975), p. 155.

7. For illustrations, see F. Campbell, Jr., following p. 100.

CHAPTER 7: "THE FINAL SOLUTION" (Esther)

1. Otto Eissfeldt, *The Old Testament: An Introduction,* translated by Peter R. Ackroyd (New York: Harper & Row, 1965), pp. 511-512.

2. *Harry James Cargas in Conversation with Elie Wiesel* (New York: Paulist Press, 1976), pp. 21-22.

3. Cf. the judicious comments in Brevard S. Childs, *Introduction to the Old Testament as Scripture* (Philadelphia: Fortress Press, 1979), pp. 603-607.

4. Herman Wouk, *This Is My God* (Garden City: Doubleday & Company, 1959), pp. 97-98.

5. Richard Siegel, Michael Strassfeld, Sharon Strassfeld, *The Jewish Catalog* (Philadelphia: The Jewish Publication Society of America, 1973), p. 136. This material is copyrighted by and used through the courtesy of The Jewish Publication Society of America.

6. Elie Wiesel, *Night,* translated by Stella Rodway (New York: Avon Books, 1969), p. 44. Translated from the French by Stella Rodway, © Les Editions De Minuit, 1958. English translation © Mac Gibbon & Kee, 1960. First published by Hill and Wang (now a division of Farrar, Straus & Giroux, Inc.).

CHAPTER 8: "AMAZING GRACE" (Jonah)

1. Martin, Luther, *Lectures on the Minor Prophets II: Jonah, Habbakkuk,* edited by Hilton C. Oswald, p. 31. FROM: LUTHER'S WORKS. Volume 19. © 1974 Concordia Publishing House. Used by permission.

2. Ibid., p. 36.

3. "Jonah" in LEDA by Aldous Huxley. Copyright 1920 by Aldous Huxley. By permission of Harper & Row, Publishers, Inc.